Imperial Germany
1890–1918

Ian Porter and
Ian D. Armour

LONGMAN
London and New York

Pearson Education Limited
Edinburgh Gate, Harlow
Essex CM20 2JE, England
and Associated Companies throughout the world.

Visit us on the World Wide Web at:
www.pearsoned.co.uk

First published 1991

Set in 10/11 point Baskerville (Linotron)

ISBN-10: 0-582-03496-5
ISBN-13: 978-0-582-03496-9

British Library Cataloguing in Publication Data
Porter, Ian
  Imperial Germany 1890–1918. – (Seminar studies in
  history).
  1. Germany, 1871–1918
  I. Title II. Armour, Ian D.   III. Series
  943.083

Library of Congress Cataloging-in-Publication Data
Porter, Ian.
  Imperial Germany, 1890–1918 / Ian Porter and Ian D. Armour.
     p.   cm. – (Seminar studies in history)
  Includes bibliographical references and index.
  ISBN 0-582-03496-5
  1. Germany – History – William II, 1888–1918. I. Armour, Ian D.
  II. Title.   III. Series.
  DD228.P67 1991
  943.08'4 – dc20   90-45617
                                                     CIP

Printed and bound by CPI Antony Rowe, Eastbourne
Transferred to digital print on demand, 2006

The publisher's policy is to use paper manufactured from sustainable forests

Contents

Contents

List of Maps

Acknowledgements

The map on page 41 is adapted from page 45 of Tony Howarth: *Twentieth Century History: The World Since 1900*, second edition by Josh Brooman, publ. Longman, 1979; the map on page 62 is adapted from page 77 of J. C. G. Röhl: *Problems and Perspectives in History – Bismarck to Hitler*, publ. Longman, 1970; the map on page vi is from D. G. Williamson: *Seminar Studies in History: Bismarck and Germany*, publ. Longman, 1986.

The authors wish to thank Zentrales Staatsarchiv, Potsdam for supplying the original for Document 31.

Seminar Studies in History
Founding Editor: Patrick Richardson

Introduction

The Seminar Studies series was conceived by Patrick Richardson, whose experience of teaching history persuaded him of the need for something more substantial than a textbook chapter but less formidable than the specialised full-length academic work. He was also convinced that such studies, although limited in length, should provide an up-to-date and authoritative introduction to the topic under discussion as well as a selection of relevant documents and a comprehensive bibliography.

Patrick Richardson died in 1979, but by that time the Seminar Studies series was firmly established, and it continues to fulfil the role he intended for it. This book, like others in the series, is therefore a living tribute to a gifted and original teacher.

Note on the System of References:
A bold number in round brackets (**5**) in the text refers the reader to the corresponding entry in the Bibliography section at the end of the book. If a name follows the bold number, this is an author of a particular essay in a collection. A bold number in square brackets, preceded by 'doc.' [**doc. 6**] refers the reader to the corresponding item in the section of Documents, which follows the main text. Items followed by an asterisk * are explained in the Glossary.

ROGER LOCKYER
General Editor

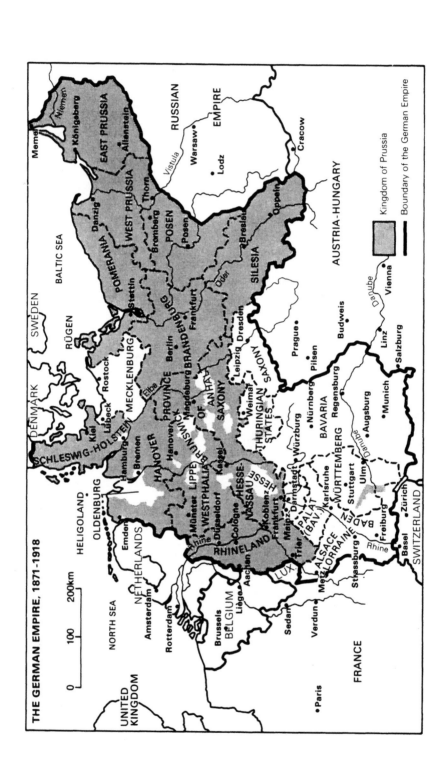

THE GERMAN EMPIRE, 1871-1918

UNITED KINGDOM

NORTH SEA

HELIGOLAND

NETHERLANDS

Amsterdam
Rotterdam

BELGIUM

Brussels
Liège

Sedan
Verdun

FRANCE

Paris

SWEDEN

BALTIC SEA

DENMARK

RÜGEN

Memel
Königsberg   EAST PRUSSIA   Allenstein

Niemen

RUSSIAN

Vistula   EMPIRE

Warsaw
Lodz

Danzig   WEST PRUSSIA   Thorn

POMERANIA   Bromberg   POSEN   Posen

Stettin

Rostock   MECKLENBURG

Lübeck   Oder

SCHLESWIG-HOLSTEIN   Kiel

Breslau

Oppeln   SILESIA

Frankfurt

BRANDENBURG   Berlin

Elbe

PROVINCE   Magdeburg   ANHALT

OLDENBURG   Emden   Hamburg   Bremen   Hanover   BRUNSWICK   SAXONY

HANOVER   Kassel   Leipzig   Dresden   Prague

LIPPE   HESSE   THURINGIAN   SAXONY   Pilsen

WESTPHALIA   NASSAU   Weimar   STATES

Münster   Cologne   Koblenz   Frankfurt   Würzburg   Nürnberg   Regensburg

Düsseldorf   Mainz   Darmstadt   BAVARIA

RHINELAND   Trier   PALAT   Karlsruhe   Stuttgart   Augsburg   Munich

Aachen   Metz   BAV.   WÜRTTEMBERG   Ulm   Danube

LUX.   ALSACE   Strassburg   BADEN   Freiburg   Zürich

LORRAINE   Basel   Zürich

SWITZERLAND

Rhine

AUSTRIA-HUNGARY

Budweis   Linz   Salzburg

Danube   Vienna

Cracow

Kingdom of Prussia

Boundary of the German Empire

0   100   200km

Part One: Background

1 The Historiography of Wilhelmine Germany

The Wilhelmine* period in Germany is vital to an understanding of German, and indeed European, history, but it is only in the last quarter-century that this has been properly appreciated, even by historians. Before 1961, when the German historian, Fritz Fischer, brought out his controversial *Griff nach der Weltmacht* (Bid for World Power) (**201**), a curious complacency reigned about events between the fall of Bismarck and the outbreak of the First World War. The only subjects which seemed to attract attention were William II (**49**), and the question of war origins; certainly very little was written on German domestic developments (**62**). Even on war origins, there was a broad consensus that the subject had been pretty thoroughly researched, and that all the European powers bore a collective responsibility for the outbreak of hostilities. For the most part, this suited German scholars. The thesis of collective responsibility helped shore up German historians' belief that the Bismarckian state was basically a good thing. Confronted, after 1945, with the need to explain the unquestionable catastrophe of Hitler and the Second World War, German historians were only too glad to draw a veil over the Wilhelmine era – a tendency epitomised in 1955 by the textbook writer who informed his readers that, in the study of the period 1914–18, 'the historian moves everywhere on firm ground' (**27**, p. 2).

Fischer's book rode rough-shod over these comfortable assumptions, sparking a controversy which has been raging bitterly ever since. In a study of the lost subject of German war aims, Fischer made a number of assertions which his fellow German historians, at least, found hard to accept. For one thing, he claimed that Germany's expansionist war aims were foreshadowed by equally aggressive and expansionist policies before 1914. War aims, Fischer wrote, were the symptoms of a planned drive for world power in evidence since the 1890s, a *Weltpolitik** which would place Germany on an equal footing with the global empires of Britain, France and Russia. Worse, not only did this aggressive policy command a significant level of popular support both before and during the First

1

World War, but it led to the decision of the German government to risk war in July 1914. For the sake of world power, Germany had consciously brought about world war (**201**).

For a German historian to saddle Germany with primary responsibility for the First World War was provocative in itself, and the reaction among the old guard of the German historical profession was one of patriotic indignation. Equally unwelcome, to Germans generally, was the suggestion of a *continuity* in German history, that the ideas and attitudes which helped produce National Socialism went back well before 1918. To that extent imperial Germany had more in common with the Third Reich than most Germans liked to admit. Fischer also insisted that German foreign policy, which led to the outbreak of war, could only be understood with reference to social, economic and domestic political factors. In asserting this, Fischer was breaking with the traditional German belief in the 'primacy of foreign policy', according to which foreign policy could be understood on its own, and determined all other aspects of a state's history. To claim otherwise was to open up a new perspective in the way Germans looked at their past (**201**; **26**; **159**).

In the 1960s a new generation of historians began to reexamine German history with new methods and assumptions. These 'revisionist' historians were bent on uncovering the domestic determinants of foreign policy. They produced, for instance, studies of the popular support for *Weltpolitik* (**3**; **153**); the role of the press in voicing that support (**177**); the influence of industrial and agrarian interest groups (**56**; **64**); the financial constraints under which the German government was operating by 1914 (**81**). A great deal was done to illustrate the sheer complexity of Wilhelmine politics and society; no one could complain, by the end of the decade, that the period 1890–1918 was still dominated by old-style diplomatic historians. Ironically, the ultimate preoccupation of all this work on domestic factors was still the explanation of that foreign policy which the domestic factors were assumed to have shaped.

By the mid-1970s, this revisionist 'primacy of domestic policy' had become so common as to be dubbed the 'new orthodoxy'. Hans-Ulrich Wehler evolved a theory of imperialism which interpreted colonial expansion as a movement conceived by the German upper and middle classes to distract the working class from socialism (**40**; **37**; **151**). Volker Berghahn depicted Wilhelmine naval policy not only as a direct challenge to British sea power, but also as designed to unite Germans behind a new object of patriotic pride. As with the search for colonies, the new fleet was more an instrument of social control than an end in itself (**131**). Nothing attracted historians more than the so-called *Sammlungspolitik** of the late 1890s, whereby a government-sponsored alliance between big business and big landowners supposedly served to 'rally' patriotic elements and limit the appeal of social democracy (**73**; **67**). The importance of the links between domestic and foreign policy, in the eyes of the revisionists, was all the greater in view of the catastrophic results of Germany's pre-war diplomacy. A principal reason for understanding imperial Germany, Wehler claimed, was the need to understand the origins of fascism (**40**).

There has certainly been no lack of historians ready to criticise individual revisionist works, but to date no coherent alternative explanation has emerged. The most severe criticisms have been reserved for the more literal interpretations of documentary evidence (**152**), or the tendency – a common enough problem in all historical debates – to concentrate only on those documents which support revisionist theories. This applies equally to the 'primacy of domestic politics'. More than one critic has pointed out the considerable gap which still exists between the elaborate theoretical constructions of many revisionists and the actual results of their often excellent detailed research (**185**; **33**; **145**).

One alternative explanation has been the idea of a 'divided society' in Germany. German industrialisation produced severe tensions between the new urban masses and a conservative elite entrenched in outmoded and inequitable political institutions. Germany 'failed' to produce a parliamentary democracy because its middle classes did not win political rights on their own, but were given them by the state. Wolfgang Mommsen, for instance, attributes the failure of Germany to avoid conflict in 1914 to its antiquated governmental system, which placed the Chancellor at the mercy of the military and conservative elites who favoured war (**164**; **27**). Recent studies reinforce this view of a sort of institutional bankruptcy, of a society in crisis, blundering into war as a direct consequence of its own internal contradictions (**13**; **160**; **184**; **20**). They also make an understanding of the Empire even more relevant to an understanding of fascism.

Even this approach has its critics. Apart from a new generation of conservative German historians, who reject the idea of continuity in German history, and attempt a return to more traditional explanations of German policy (**36**; **176**; **31**), the more recent contributors to the debate on Wilhelmine Germany are perhaps best represented by Geoff Eley and David Blackbourn (**24**; **23**; **46**; **15**;

16). Concepts like *Sammlungspolitik* and social imperialism, wrote Eley, 'seemed to impute too much unity and coherence to the empire's "ruling elites"' (**22**, p. 10). Eley and Blackbourn also question whether the stress laid by so many scholars on the 'peculiarities' of the Germans, on the supposed 'failure' of German society to develop 'normal' parliamentary institutions, is entirely historical. Neither denies the element of continuity; but to some extent the strains imposed by industrialisation were to be expected, and would have come regardless of the nature of German political institutions. German history, in other words, is less unique than we are accustomed to think; certainly more work needs to be done comparing it with other societies (**16**; **22**). Even more recently Thomas Nipperdey has also reemphasised the complexity of Wilhelmine society and its more progressive elements. Not only was Germany comparable to other societies, it was segmented along religious, regional and social lines; it was a pluralist society, with many competing social groups; it was reformist, with advanced social legislation; its press was capable of being highly critical; and it was gradually changing, despite the imperfections of the political system (**34**).

2 The House that Bismarck Built

The German Empire was created in 1871, so it is impossible to understand its development after 1890 without some knowledge of its brief history and institutions. Its very nature gave rise to serious problems. Even Otto von Bismarck, the first imperial Chancellor, had difficulties with the machinery he set up; after his forced departure in 1890 the structural weaknesses of the Empire became increasingly obvious.

Germany's 'unification', strictly speaking, never took place (**79**; **51**). Austria had been excluded from a say in German affairs after 1866, and the war of 1870–71 against France made possible the accession of the south German states to the new Empire. But this realisation of the dream of unity was intentionally limited. It specifically excluded the German-speaking, but Catholic, population of the Austrian Empire. It was also flawed by the inclusion of sizeable non-German or otherwise alienated minorities: Poles in the east (**84**; **124**), Danes in the north (**96**), the annexed provinces of Alsace and Lorraine in the west (**121**). There had been considerable opposition by some Germans to the idea of submitting to Prussian hegemony, especially among the largely Catholic population of the south German states.

The constitution of 1871 not only reflected this disunity but actually helped perpetuate it. Bismarck's aim in drafting the constitution was to preserve Prussian dominance, and this meant deliberately limiting the power of the central government. The result was a state which was federal in the true sense of the word: certain very strictly defined powers were reserved to the centre; but all else was left to the twenty-five individual states of the Empire, which retained their own princes, constitutions and governments (**20**; **34**; **25**).

At the head of the federal government was the Emperor, who was also the King of Prussia. His position demonstrates that, although Germany was a constitutional state, it was hardly a parliamentary one, because the monarch was in no real sense accountable to an elected assembly. On the contrary, it was stressed that the constitution of 1871 was *granted* to the German people (**28**). The Emperor had wide powers. He appointed the head of the imperial government, the Chancellor, who was responsible to him alone. He had the final say in all matters of foreign policy, including the power to declare war and conclude peace. He exercised supreme command in time of war over the armed forces of all states of the Empire, and the war ministry and general staff remained Prussian and were responsible to him, not to the Chancellor, much less parliament (**132**). Article 68 of the constitution gave the Emperor explicit power to subordinate the civilian authorities to the military in wartime. This was invoked in 1914, and made possible the military dictatorship which ran Germany in the last two years of the First World War (**209**).

Beneath the Emperor was the Federal Council or *Bundesrat*. This was made up of delegates appointed by the state governments, and was in theory the supreme constitutional body. All proposals for legislation to be laid before the federal parliament had to be approved by the Council, and any amendments by parliament had to be accepted by it. The Federal Council was also the only means of amending the constitution. In reality, Prussia's voice remained decisive: Prussia had seventeen out of the fifty-eight seats in the Federal Council, and no constitutional change could be made without Prussian consent. Nor could the Federal Council make fundamental alterations affecting the armed forces, or imperial finance, if the Prussian government opposed them. Its role quickly dwindled to that of a mere rubber-stamp for imperial legislation (**28**).

Instead, the principal direction of affairs was left to the Chancellor, whose office became, next to the Emperor, the real power-house of government in imperial Germany. The Chancellor almost always filled the post of Prussian Minister President; and as Chancellor he presided over the Federal Council, and could appear before parliament to explain policy if he so chose. The executive branches of the federal government evolved not as ministries, but as offices (*Ämter*) of the Chancellor's department, headed by 'secretaries of state' (**28**; **32**). In addition to foreign policy, the federal authority extended to commercial affairs, tariffs, transport and communications, coinage, weights and measures, and other matters of common federal concern (**86**).

At the bottom was the imperial parliament, the *Reichstag*, 397 deputies elected every five years by universal manhood suffrage and secret ballot. Universal suffrage was not as revolutionary as it seemed, since genuine working-class representation was made almost impossible by stipulating that deputies should receive no salary, a provision only reversed in 1906 (**28**). The Reichstag had the right to debate and approve legislation, but not generally to initiate it. It had some ability to control the imperial government by amending government bills, but the Chancellor could always dissolve a Reichstag that was too obstructive. The Chancellor and his subordinates were not members of the Reichstag, nor were they responsible to it. In the eyes of some historians, this amounted to parliamentary impotence (**40**; **13**). Others, however, have seen a gradual strengthening of the Reichstag's position after 1900 (**25**; **70**; **75**; **72**).

One of the central weaknesses of imperial Germany was the vulnerability of the Chancellor. He might be independent of the Reichstag, but he was wholly dependent on the Emperor's favour. Under the elderly William I (1871–88) this tended to be obscured, since Bismarck's forceful character created the illusion of a strong position (**79**). But when William II chose to take an active part in government, then the Chancellor really had little choice but to agree or get out. The fact that William's interventions in policy-making were both incompetent and erratic was neither here nor there; his control over the appointment or dismissal of the Chancellor was absolute. This was a recipe for chaos at the top (**49**; **67**; **40**).

The other great weakness of the Empire was the often unappreciated extent of states' rights. Particularism, or loyalty to individual states, was strong in Germany, especially in the Catholic south. The state governments kept exclusive legislative authority in such matters as education, health, and law and order. Some of them retained their own armies, although these were subordinate to the Emperor and the Prussian military authorities, especially in time of war. But the real Achilles heel of the Empire was finance (**81**). The federal government received the income from customs and from internal duties on sugar, salt, tobacco and other consumer items, and from the various postal and telegraph systems of the Empire. There was, however, no national income tax. The individual states collected their own taxes, and the constitution even stipulated that the revenues due to the central authorities should also be collected by the states. This defect was extremely difficult to reform, because of the structure of the constitution; and yet the mounting expenditure of the Wilhelmine regime, especially on the armed forces, made a solution increasingly urgent. Well before the First World War, the Empire was facing a full-scale financial crisis (**13**; **81**).

There has been much debate on the role of Prussia as a factor hampering real German unification, with some historians arguing that Germany was 'Prussianised' (**17**), while others see Prussia as being gradually absorbed into Germany (**66**). Certainly the Prussian influence, right down to 1918, was no fiction: the Prussian government dominated the Federal Council; it directed foreign policy; and it controlled the armed forces. But the federation in a sense outgrew the limited role assigned to it (**34**). Particularism remained strong and perpetuated differing loyalties; but a real national consciousness can be seen evolving by the turn of the century, most noticeably among the middle classes (**46**).

Part of the problem with Prussia was that its three-class electoral system remained a highly restrictive one. Deputies to the Prussian *Landtag** were not elected directly. Instead, the electors in each constituency were divided into three classes according to the amount of tax they paid. Each class chose representatives, who together selected the deputies. This gave a disproportionate political influence to the upper and middle classes. In 1908, for instance, the most conservative party, with 16 per cent of the vote, could win 212 seats, while the mass-based *SPD**, with 23 per cent, won only eight. Nowhere else in the Empire was the traditional aristocratic and military elite more firmly entrenched (**25**; **220**; **49**).

Bismarck left a troubled legacy, in that his general political approach helped shape the tactics of his successors (**51**; **79**). Before the Reichstag he constantly emphasised his responsibility to the Emperor alone. His tendency to see threatening groups in society, hostile to the state – the Catholics, the Poles, then the socialists – and his belief that against such groups any counter-measures were justifiable, also characterised the politics of the following period. It was a fundamentally divisive attitude, and it helped keep alienated the two largest mass parties in the Reichstag (**59**; **68**).

The Empire was also subject to quite exceptional economic and social stresses. German industrialisation had been in full swing since the middle of the century; it had been particularly marked in Prussia, which was one reason why Prussia assumed so prominent a role in unification (**120**). By 1890 Germany was the major industrial and military power on the European continent, a fact which was recognised both in Germany and abroad (**18**). This potential was so obvious that it spawned domestic pressure for a more ambitious foreign and colonial policy; the desire for world power status, with world power economic opportunities, was an essential part of government policy under William II (**153**; **177**; **178**).

Part Two: Narration and Analysis

3 Domestic Politics, 1890–1914

The road to 'personal rule', 1890–97

William II, in 1890, longed to escape from Bismarck's oppressive shadow, but was a lightweight by comparison. Weak, emotionally unstable, liable to fits of bizarre rage and hysteria, the Emperor glorified his Prussian ancestors and Prussia's military traditions, was happiest in the company of soldiers and fawning favourites, and despised civilians, politicians and socialists (**8**; **9**). He had little political ability, but was filled with 'a grandiose belief in his own importance' (**11**, p. 36) [**doc. 1a, b**]. Above all, William was determined to establish what he thought would be 'personal rule', in which ministers did *his* bidding, without regard to parliament or public opinion (**49**; **67**), but was neither hard-working nor consistent enough to direct policy in any practical sense. Instead, he was 'the one constant, unavoidable, unpredictable factor with which all statesmen in Berlin, for better or worse, had to reckon' (**8**, p. 261).

One of the reasons that made it easy for William to dismiss Bismarck was that the Chancellor's support in the Reichstag had disintegrated. His successors found it increasingly necessary to have a parliamentary grouping they could work with; and the character of individual parties assumed greater significance.

On the right, the German Conservatives (*DKP**) represented the interests of the aristocracy and large landowners, especially in Prussia; their main strength remained in the Prussian Landtag rather than the Reichstag (**63**; **66**). The Free Conservatives or *Reichspartei** were more mixed, with both industrialists and agrarians among their supporters. Also basically conservative, although progressive in some matters of social reform, was the Catholic Centre Party (*Zentrum**), which existed primarily to defend the interests of Catholics (**68**; **42**). The National Liberal Party represented the wealthier middle class, the party of constitutional liberties and free enterprise, and tended to side with the conservative parties (**71**; **78**). A radical off-shoot of National Liberalism, the German Free Thought Party (*DFP**), took a more critical view of government, especially in military affairs. In 1893, these left-liberals split into three squabbling factions, and only re-united in 1910 (**71**; **54**). On the left, the SPD spoke for the German working class; in 1890 it had only just been released from the restrictions of the anti-socialist law (**61**). The Poles, Danes, Alsace-Lorrainers and Guelphs* returned their own representatives to the Reichstag; and from 1890 a small number of explicitly anti-Semitic deputies was a permanent feature of each parliament. The Conservatives, National Liberals, left-liberals and Centre all regularly polled a million votes or more, but it was the meteoric rise of the SPD which became a phobia of the imperial government, since socialism was held to threaten the very fabric of the state.

William's choice to replace Bismarck as Chancellor was General Leo von Caprivi. The Emperor probably thought Caprivi would do as he was told (**62**). In fact, Caprivi was an intelligent, highly principled man with a mind of his own, and decidedly progressive views for a general. He thought a 'new course' was necessary in governing the Reich: less autocratic control of the government by the Chancellor, more initiative from ministers and more cooperation with the Reichstag; social reform that would reconcile the working class to the established order; and lower tariffs which would improve Germany's export trade and enable German industry to expand (**62**; **77**).

Caprivi had some initial successes, in part because he allowed the anti-socialist law to lapse, and thus ensured the cooperation of both the Social Democrats and the Centre for some of his policies. The Social Law of 1891 outlawed Sunday working and the employment of children under thirteen. Further legislation set up a compulsory industrial arbitration procedure, involving both employers and employees (**85**).

Most significant was the reform of the Tariff Act. Caprivi was concerned at the damage high protective customs duties were doing to both trade and foreign relations [**doc. 2**]. The trade treaties which Caprivi steered through the Reichstag between 1891 and 1894 offered Germany's trading partners a swap: in return for easier access to foreign markets for German goods, Germany reduced tariffs on foodstuffs, notably grain. Because this meant a reduction in the price of food the Caprivi treaties were approved by all political parties with the significant exception of the Conservatives (**77**; **41**). In 1893 a group of landowners formed their own pressure group, the Farmers' League (*BdL**), to fight the treaties. The BdL rapidly developed a bitter, mass-based campaign against what it called 'tariff socialism' (**76**; **64**; **66**) [**doc. 3**].

Caprivi fell a victim to the strength of the interests opposed to his policies. His government had no natural majority in the Reichstag: with the Conservatives alienated by the reduction in grain tariffs, each legislative measure was dependent on ever-shifting coalitions.

Caprivi's efforts at decentralising government only served to breed intrigue against him. In 1892 Caprivi broke with Bismarck's tradition of holding both the chancellorship and the office of Prussian Minister President, and Count Botho zu Eulenburg, a reactionary landowner, became head of the Prussian government. Eulenburg's cousin, Philipp zu Eulenburg, was already a personal favourite of the Emperor, and for years fed William's delusions of 'personal rule' by every form of gross flattery (**67**). To the Eulenburgs and their allies, Caprivi's policies were anathema, and they tempted William with plans for a *Staatsstreich**. An anti-socialist Subversion Bill would be submitted to the Reichstag by Eulenburg as Caprivi's successor, and its rejection would furnish the pretext for ruling without parliament. Caprivi managed to persuade William of the dangers of a *Staatsstreich*, but he clearly no longer enjoyed the Emperor's confidence. William, unable to choose between Eulenburg and the Chancellor, characteristically ended by dismissing both (**62**).

The new Chancellor, Prince Chlodwig zu Hohenlohe-Schillingsfürst, was truly a stopgap appointment: an elderly Bavarian, he proved to be more obstinate than expected, but was definitely no leader. His chancellorship has been described as 'government by procrastination' (**50**). Hohenlohe imposed no overall control, although he resumed the Prussian minister presidency; and there was still no obvious government coalition in the Reichstag. Most of Hohenlohe's energies were devoted to coping with the Emperor's alarming flights of fancy. These came most repeatedly in the form of inflammatory speeches and demands for anti-socialist legislation [**doc. 1a**]. A new Subversion Bill was duly introduced in the Reichstag in 1895, and duly voted down. It was clearly impossible to pass anti-socialist laws; but conversely the Reichstag could play no role beyond this purely negative one (**85**).

In this situation the reality behind the socialist bogy which so exercised the mind of the Emperor is worth examining. The SPD congress at Erfurt in 1891 had re-affirmed its principles as a party of revolution, and in the 1893 elections it polled more votes than any other party. Yet in practice the SPD in the Wilhelmine era was

11

becoming less revolutionary. The party leader, August Bebel, was alive to the possibilities of achieving social reform through parliamentary action (**60**). Other leaders, like the theorist Eduard Bernstein, or the Bavarian Georg Vollmar, made clear their belief in a 'gradual socialisation' (**155**) [**doc. 4**]. There is little doubt that this 'revisionism' reflected the opinions of the party rank-and-file, who were broadly content to concentrate on bread-and-butter issues and were just as patriotic as any other group of Germans (**61**). The consistent refusal of the imperial government to acknowledge this fact made a fateful contribution to the political stalemate of Wilhelmine Germany. The SPD was heavily represented in the Reichstag, but no government could even think of turning to it for support. The chancellorships of Bülow and Bethmann Hollweg reflected the increasing difficulty of finding a stable government majority.

The ascendancy of Bülow, 1897–1909

The stalemate of the years 1894–97 was seemingly broken when William II made a number of appointments which, he hoped, would finally inaugurate 'personal rule'. William was frustrated by the reluctance of Hohenlohe, backed by survivors from the Caprivi period, to implement his will. Yet it was only when suitable replacements had emerged, who promised more than ordinary skill in handling the Reichstag, while being at the same time committed to doing the Emperor's bidding, that William deemed it safe to act. Hohenlohe could be left in office as a venerable figurehead, masking the real wielders of power (**67**; **10**; **9**).

Foremost among these new men was Count Bernhard von Bülow, appointed Reich Foreign Secretary and later Chancellor. Bülow was a clever professional diplomat, with a special talent for appearing all things to all men. He was primarily interested in foreign policy, where he had the same vision of Germany's imperial destiny as William II (**178**; **179**). In domestic politics he was a believer in conciliation, but identified closely with the conservative landowning class from which he sprang. Introduced to the Emperor by Eulenburg, Bülow rapidly built up a false image of himself in the Emperor's mind as a political strongman (**57**).

Bülow was only one of a group of forceful personalities who came into prominence in 1897. The Prussian Finance Minister, Johannes von Miquel, was a deeply conservative thinker, and one of the chief proponents of *Sammlungspolitik*. The Reich Secretary of the Interior, Count Arthur von Posadowsky-Wehner, was brought in as another strongman who would force the necessary anti-socialist legislation through the Reichstag. And Admiral Alfred von Tirpitz became Navy Secretary, with the specific brief of overturning the Reichstag's opposition to a naval building programme. All three were to make distinctive contributions to the domestic scene.

At the core of government strategy was supposed to lie a unified political concept called *Sammlungspolitik*. Certainly ministers like Bülow and Miquel spoke of the need to 'rally' patriotic forces in German society behind the government [**doc. 5**]. A distinction must nowadays be drawn, however, between the meanings ascribed to *Sammlungspolitik* by historians (**40**; **73**; **131**; **22**), and what, if anything, it meant to people in the Wilhelmine period [**doc. 6**]. Miquel was clearly harking back to the Bismarckian coalition of conservative and liberal parties which had up to then eluded William II. In contrast to Bismarck, however, Miquel, no less than Bülow, Posadowsky and Tirpitz, realised that no *Sammlung* could be effective without the participation of the Centre (**22**). To that extent politics was beginning to reflect a genuine need for government majorities in the Reichstag; even 'personal rule' could not function without parliamentary allies.

It appears impossible to regard the navy as playing a central role in *Sammlungspolitik* (**22**). On the contrary, ministers knew perfectly well that the landowners or agrarians, one of the groups they wished most to unite behind them, had deep-rooted objections to what they called the 'horrible fleet' (**49**, p. 268), which they rightly regarded as an agent of further industrialisation. But ministers *had* to push on with naval construction, because William II had personally made it government policy [**doc. 1c**]. If the government did make offers of protective tariffs to the conservatives in return for their support for the fleet in the Reichstag, this was probably no more than political 'log-rolling' (**41**, p. 229); the support of industry could be taken for granted (**133**). However, both Bülow and Miquel saw foreign policy as a vital ingredient in *Sammlungspolitik* [**doc. 5**].

The difficulties experienced in rallying a wide range of parties and interest groups make a nonsense of the thesis that *Sammlung* was the 'ideology' of the ruling classes in Wilhelmine Germany (**73**, p. 13). Part of the problem was the conflicting influence exerted on the Reichstag parties by a number of powerful extra-parliamentary pressure groups. Heavy industry was represented by the Central Association of German Industrialists (*CVDI**) (**56**); whereas the Industrialists' League (*BdI**) spoke for light and export manufacturers. Many heavy industrialists could see a point in joining forces with the agrarians, since the market within Germany for their products, such as steel, would be safeguarded by high tariffs. They were also by nature conservative and, as employers, anxious to combat socialism. But politically such people were divided between the conservative parties and the National Liberals; and the National Liberal Party in turn was split between CVDI interests and BdI ones. Many National Liberals were not convinced of the need for higher tariffs; if they were BdI members they opposed tariffs outright, since their export trade depended on low tariffs.

In the agrarian camp an even greater gap yawned between the moderates, represented by the German Agricultural Council (*DLR**), which wanted modest tariff increases, and the hard right, demagogic Farmers' League. The BdL attacked anyone not in favour of massive tariff increases, and their intransigence made them impossible as allies (**76**; **64**). The *Sammlung* eventually cobbled together in time for the Reichstag elections of June 1898 was thus an uneasy alliance of the conservative parties and the National Liberals, with the Centre holding aloof. It was also a resounding failure, since only the Centre and the SPD made any gains (**22**).

The government was able to secure Reichstag support for the two Navy Laws of 1898 and 1900, and the Tariff Law of 1902. Tirpitz proved to be a brilliant manager of the Reichstag. Equally important, he was adept at orchestrating extra-parliamentary support for the navy in a way that political parties found hard to ignore. In political terms the popularity of the navy really did produce support for the government: when Tirpitz got his first Navy Act passed in March 1898, it was also with the support of a majority of Centre deputies (**144**). The navy continued to be popular. It was only later that the financial implications began to sink in.

The upward revision of Germany's tariffs was a sterner test. The whole purpose of *Sammlung* as formulated by Miquel in 1897 had been to ensure support for such revision and thus secure the prosperity and survival of the Prussian landowning class (**22**). Bülow, Chancellor after 1900, was wholeheartedly in agreement with this goal. The extreme protectionists, however, were not easy people to help. Even the substantial tariff increases which Bülow offered were not enough to pacify them. In the end the new tariff law was passed by a combination of moderate Conservatives, the National Liberals and the Centre. The diehard agrarians found themselves sharing their defeat with the left-liberals and the SPD, who opposed protection because of the higher food prices which it was bound to entail. After 1902, Bülow's fragile coalition of industrialists and moderate agrarians proved more and more difficult to sustain (**41**; **64**; **76**; **66**).

Posadowsky was also finding support for legislation, although hardly in the way he had originally intended. He came to office resolved to turn the clock back with rigorous anti-socialist measures, but discovered there was hardly any parliamentary backing for repressive legislation. When he laid before the Reichstag in 1899 a bill threatening prison sentences for strike action which could be deemed harmful to 'public security', it was rejected out of hand by all parties except the DKP and Free Conservatives. Re-submitted at William's insistence, it was again decisively voted down. Posadowsky had enough political sense to realise that, if the appeal of socialism were to be limited at all, it could not be through repression [**doc. 7**]. After 1899 he aimed instead at extending social security. In this he found the support of the Centre vital, since the conservatives and the National Liberals regarded social legislation with distaste. In 1900 the period for which workers could claim accident insurance was lengthened; in 1901 industrial arbitration courts were made compulsory for towns with a population of more than 20,000; in 1903 health insurance was extended, and further controls imposed on child labour. These measures were passed with the assistance of the Centre, the left-liberals and even the SPD (**85**).

The political as well as the financial costs of Bülow's other policies, however, were now becoming apparent. In the 1903 elections, the parties which had gained most from the 1902 tariff were by and large losers. The Centre continued to hold the parliamentary balance, but the SPD's vote jumped from two to three million, with the party gaining eighty-one seats. In the face of this the Centre felt increasingly obliged to shift ground. Some Centre deputies rightly feared that Catholic workers were turning to the SPD (**14**); and they were aware that their support for the government had not gained much for Catholic interests. The more populist wing of the Centre, led by Matthias Erzberger, was more critical of the government, and, in 1905, even joined the SPD in voting down increases in the military budget (**81**). Erzberger also made a series of sensational attacks on the government's policy in German South West Africa (today's Namibia), accusing it of incompetence, financial irregularities and brutal treatment of the natives (**48**).

Financial problems, however, did most to undermine Bülow's chancellorship. The government simply could not afford all its projects: a strong standing army, the acquisition and administration of unprofitable colonies, above all the enormously expensive navy.

Since 1900 the Reich treasury had been operating at a deficit (**81**). Bülow, however, was not the sort of man to tackle a problem head-on if it could be shelved until further notice. He was aware that, whereas the SPD and the left-liberals opposed attempts to increase government income by raising indirect taxes on consumer items, the parties of the right were equally hostile to an inheritance tax, which would hit landowners and the wealthy. It was not until 1905–06 that Bülow made an effort to win new powers of taxation, but his proposed inheritance tax was so mangled·by the conservatives as to be valueless, while the left and the Centre obstructed indirect taxes.

The Centre's opposition, combined with their criticism of colonial policy, decided Bülow on a decisive break with them. In doing this he hoped to consolidate the support of the conservatives and National Liberals. Posadowsky and his social reform policies were dropped and the Reichstag elections of 1907 were conducted on a nationalistic platform which, in the short term, solved Bülow's problems (**44**). The number of SPD seats was halved, and while the Centre's position remained unchanged, the parties of the right made sufficient gains for the formation of the 'Bülow Bloc', totalling over 200 members. But the 'Bloc' was essentially artificial. When Bülow renewed his tax proposals in 1909, he found himself facing the same situation as in 1905–06, with the added twist that the parties which opposed the inheritance tax most were those on which he relied for his majority (**81**).

Meanwhile, in the autumn of 1908, Bülow destroyed his one essential prop by alienating William II. The uproar over the *Daily Telegraph* interview, in which the Emperor allowed his bombastic comments on Anglo-German relations to be published in a British newspaper, was the severest constitutional crisis of William's reign. By intimating that the majority of Germans were anti-British, in contrast to his own friendship for Britain, William made himself vastly unpopular with conservative and nationalist opinion in Germany. The *Daily Telegraph* affair produced concerted demands in the press and Reichstag for a curb on William's behaviour. Bülow allied himself with his master's critics, in that he evaded the issue of his own responsibility and forced William to give an undertaking to moderate his conduct in future. From then on William was inclined to welcome any excuse to be rid of the man he felt had betrayed him (**43**; **168**; **9**; **10**).

The importance of this was demonstrated when Bülow presented his financial reforms to the Reichstag in 1909 (**81**). The Bülow Bloc promptly split wide open. The conservatives rejected the inheritance tax, and found a willing ally in the Centre, which had not forgiven Bülow for his attacks during the 1907 elections (**44**). Apart from the inheritance tax, the government's proposals were largely accepted, as amended by this 'Blue-Black Bloc' of Conservatives and Centre; but Bülow, his parliamentary majority in tatters, chose to resign rather than accept this (**81**; **48**). Bülow's legacy was one of crisis: the hole in the Reich's finances had not been plugged, and there seemed to be no common ground between Reichstag and government.

Governing 'from issue to issue', 1909–14

Theobald von Bethmann Hollweg, who became Chancellor in July 1909, was a bureaucrat who had risen by his obvious honesty and administrative competence. He was a logical choice in a situation where the government was more than ever involved in a delicate balancing act between conflicting parties and interests. The Chancellor claimed in December 1909 that since the Reichstag, by wrecking Bülow's tax proposals, had renounced its chance to participate in government, he would not rely on any party or group of parties. In practice, Bethmann Hollweg's administration was too conservative to be able to ignore the Conservatives and National Liberals, and not liberal enough to placate the left-liberals, let alone the SPD. It was too traditionalist to attempt any truly radical initiatives, but at the same time had to cope with the 'enhanced self-consciousness' of a Reichstag encouraged by its success against Bülow (**164**, p. 29).

The political situation remained highly fluid. The Blue-Black coalition was no more stable than the Conservative-National Liberal alliance before it. On the other hand, the left-liberals were beginning to see that cooperation with the SPD might make electoral sense. Even in the National Liberal Party there was some evidence of dissatisfaction with the way the Conservatives opposed all reform (**71**). But it was the right-wing nationalist pressure groups which maintained the highest profile in this period of parliamentary deadlock. By 1910 the more reactionary elements of the CVDI were establishing links with the wild men of the right, the BdL (**56**). Extreme nationalist associations included the Pan-German League (*ADV**), which mobilised support for defence, for an aggressive foreign and colonial policy, and for a strong line against dissident national

17

minorities (**87**); and the 'League for the Furtherance of Germandom in the Eastern Marches', known as the *Hakatisten* (*HKT**), which urged a repressive anti-Polish policy (**124**; **95**).

Before the next elections in January 1912, Bethmann Hollweg undertook a series of measures which he hoped would give the impression of movement. Most controversial were the long-awaited proposals for reform of the Prussian suffrage, laid before the *Landtag* in February 1910. Yet the suffrage bill hardly attacked the root of the problem. Bethmann Hollweg was more concerned with arresting than promoting democratisation which, he declared, 'in all countries contributed to the brutalizing and diluting of political morals' (**55**, p. 78). The bill aimed only at a slight strengthening of the educated middle class among the electorate. Even this was too radical for the Conservatives and Centre, while not enough for the other parties. Rather than amend the bill, Bethmann Hollweg simply withdrew it in May 1910 (**27**).

Two nationalities issues also illustrated the political costs of Bethmann Hollweg's 'half-hearted reformism' (**27**). Wishing to relax the policy of 'Germanising' Prussian Poles, the government immediately ran into the outrage of the Pan-Germans and the *Hakatisten*. Bethmann Hollweg finally promised to begin expropriation of Polish estates, in accordance with a law passed under Bülow. This alienated all parties except the Conservatives, and the result, in 1913, was the first vote of censure against a Chancellor in the history of the Empire (**95**; **84**). In Alsace-Lorraine, in 1911, Bethmann Hollweg introduced a constitution, ending direct rule from Berlin. He had originally intended a restricted suffrage for elections to the local *Landtag*, to avoid unfavourable comparisons with Prussia; the provinces only got universal suffrage because of an amendment passed by the Reichstag (**121**).

Finance, however, remained the real stumbling-block. Backed by his treasury secretary, Adolf Wermuth, Bethmann Hollweg managed to hold back government expenditure for two years. For Wermuth, retrenchment was the only option: there must be no extra military spending until the 1912 elections had clarified the situation (**81**). Wermuth's austerity had some effect: in 1909–12 the imperial government's debt was reduced by 90 million marks, although it still totalled a crushing 489,000,000,000 (**86**).

In the 1912 elections, Bülow's chickens came home to roost. The refusal, in 1909, to accept any meaningful reform, while increasing indirect taxes, cost both the Conservatives and the Centre votes. Helped by continuing high tariffs, the cost of living had risen, and the result was a massive boost in support for the SPD to over four million votes. One in three German electors had voted Social Democrat (**61**). The Progressives and the SPD together could conceivably exercise a majority in the Reichstag in the not so distant future. But this only heightened the sense of parliamentary stalemate, since for the government reliance on an SPD-based majority was unthinkable. It was in these circumstances that people began to ask if the Reich was any longer governable at all. Bethmann Hollweg could only re-affirm his intention of seeking majorities 'from issue to issue', without relying on any fixed grouping of parties (**55**, p. 91).

In February 1912 both the Navy Office and the War Ministry demanded large increases in expenditure. Both departments had the enthusiastic support of the Emperor (**143**), and popular pressure was exerted on the government by defence associations (**46**). Wermuth's solution to the sudden strain on the imperial treasury was forthright: funds of this magnitude could only be raised by means of a proper inheritance tax [**doc. 8**]. The Prussian government at once declared its opposition, and Bethmann Hollweg, unwilling to face the growing impatience of William II and Tirpitz at the delay, backed down. He proposed instead a tax on spirits. This was only postponing the issue, for the Reichstag, led by the Liberals and Centre, accepted only on condition that the government introduced 'a general property tax' in the spring of 1913 (**13**; **81**).

Late in 1912, an appeal for even more expenditure was made by the generals. Their proposals amounted to 'the biggest army bill in German history' (**20**, p. 296). This second Army Bill succeeded where years of political strife had failed: it forced both Bethmann Hollweg and most of the parties to recognise that some form of inheritance tax was inevitable. Government and Reichstag, in this case, were convinced by the army's estimate of the threat to national security; even the SPD supported the eventual tax package, anxious to demonstrate the patriotism of its working-class voters in the face of the perceived danger from tsarist Russia, and only the Conservatives voted against it. The resulting direct property tax was also the first time since 1871 that the federal states had agreed to an alteration in the tax structure of the Empire. Despite the inheritance tax, however, the national debt was back up to 490,000,000,000 marks by 1913; and the deficit for that year was 400 million marks (**13**; **86**).

The conservative classes and interest groups in imperial Germany were by now deeply hostile not only to the left, but also to the government, which they felt had failed them. Right-wing leaders were seriously considering the idea of war, not only as salutary in itself for German society, but also as a splendid excuse for crushing Social Democracy. This concept of an 'escape forwards' has been treated by some historians as if it were the deciding element in German politics in the period 1909–14 (**40**); it is often forgotten that the influence exercised by some of its advocates was debatable, if it existed at all (**164**; **189**). It is also true that Germany need not have been 'ungovernable' if the government had been prepared to cooperate with parliament; its inability, or disinclination, to do so made 'governability' seem a real problem.

4 Social and Economic Developments

Germany as an industrial power

Germany's high and sustained rate of industrial growth was the dominant feature of the European economic landscape throughout the period 1871–1914 [**doc. 9**]. It was much more persistent than that of either France or Britain, and was rivalled on the Continent only by that of Russia and, outside Europe, by the United States (**97**). By 1890, Germany had achieved the decisive shift to an industrial economy: the number of people employed in industry was more than in agriculture (**40; 108**). But the most pronounced growth and change, and hence social stress, came in the period 1890–1910. On the eve of the First World War Germany produced two-thirds of European steel, and 20 per cent more electrical energy than Britain, France and Italy combined; mined more than half the coal; and had the biggest cotton industry on the Continent. In the new industries of chemicals and electrics, German industry led the field [**doc. 10**].

The foundations of this growth were to some extent common to all industrialising economies; but some were peculiar to Germany. A large population provided both the necessary work-force and the domestic market; and Germany's population, almost 50 million in 1890, had jumped to 65 million by 1910, in part due to the sharp decline in emigration after 1890 (**108; 82**). There was an abundance of good agricultural land, and the increasing productivity of both the large landed estates east of the River Elbe and the independent peasant farmers of the west and south-west was an essential ingredient in the general economic boom, even if Germany remained a net importer of basic foodstuffs (**86**). By 1914 German agriculture, in terms of yield per hectare, was the most productive in the world. In 1912 Germany produced 2,260 kilogrammes of wheat per hectare, compared with 1,070 in the USA; 1,850 kg of rye, compared with the USA's 1,060; and 15,030 kg of potatoes, compared with 7,620 in the USA (**86**). Rootcrops like potatoes and sugar beet, which accounted for almost 20 per cent of arable land by 1913, were the single most important cause of this revolution in German agriculture. They facilitated more rapid crop rotation; encouraged greater use of fertilisers and machinery; provided additional fodder for livestock; and led to more business-like cultivation of the land, with heavy reliance on large numbers of cheap seasonal workers. This had an effect on the chemical and machine-making industries, and on meat and dairy production. It increased internal migration and hence the influx of foreign agricultural labourers into the Prussian East (**116**).

Industrial raw materials had increasingly to be imported, although the Empire was well provided with the basics of coal and iron ore. It also possessed many of the resources for the chemicals industry, such as potassium salts and coal tar. Equally important was the existence of an extensive transport network: the railways of the various German states were essentially complete by about 1880; and much attention was also devoted to improving the canal and river system. This stimulated the shipbuilding industry, which in turn facilitated the expansion of German overseas trade; by 1908 the total tonnage of the German merchant navy was second only to Britain's (**98**). A sound financial basis for industry was also available through the capital accumulated by established banking firms; and after 1890 German banks not only grew phenomenally but also maintained close links with industry (**115**).

Wilhelmine Germany differed from its neighbours in the scale and concentration of its economic and industrial muscle. The new Germany simply constituted a much bigger market than any other industrial European state. It made possible the establishment of a single German currency, agreement on common weights and measures, and the improvement of transport and communications (**86; 97; 108**).

The sheer size of German firms resulted in the economy developing on a large scale. As German firms, financial as well as industrial, grew bigger and bigger, they found it increasingly profitable to agree with one another on a division of the market rather than to compete. These cartels were understandings either to share the market; or to fix prices; or to fix total volumes of production, with each firm receiving a 'quota'; or to share profits (**107**). Thus, in the Ruhr coalfield, ten giant collieries produced some 60 per cent of output by 1910, of which 86 per cent was regulated by cartel agreement. In iron and steel, huge firms like Krupp and Thyssen dominated entire cities, such as Essen. The market in chemicals was cornered by two main groups of companies, F. Bayer & Co. and the Hoechst

Farbenwerke chain, who organised a cartel in 1904. The electrical industry was divided up by 1914 between the Siemens group and the Allgemeine Elektrizitäts-Gesellschaft (AEG), operating a cartel from 1908. Similar arrangements obtained in the world of shipbuilding and shipping, textiles and so on. Even the four great banks which provided most of the investment capital for German industry – the Dresdner Bank, the Deutsche Bank, the Darmstädter Bank and the Diskontogesellschaft – not only ran their own cartel agreements but actively promoted cartels in industry (**107**; **30**). Economic historians are doubtful as to whether this restriction of competition had a positive effect on the economy, although there was a gradual rise in living standards (**86**; **98**; **108**).

Of direct relevance to both industry and agriculture was the protectionist policy pursued by the imperial government after 1879. By 1890, protective tariffs had become a foreign trade liability: other countries, particularly in eastern Europe, had retaliated against Germany's tariffs by imposing their own. The Caprivi government's trade treaties reduced duties, and had the added merit of fixing tariffs for the next twelve years (**77**). Arguably, it was these treaties which, by rejuvenating trade, 'helped to make Germany the leading industrial nation in Europe by 1900' (**19**, p. 176). The Bülow tariff of 1902, however, reversed this policy for purely political reasons. Economic historians point out that the justification for protection was minimal: high tariffs did not necessarily benefit all German industrial manufacturers either at home or abroad; and they undoubtedly kept the price of foodstuffs, especially grain, artificially high (**98**; **108**; **30**). What is not disputed is that protection was of great assistance to the landowners in preserving their incomes and hence their social and political influence.

Nevertheless the German economy remained strong right down to 1914 and throughout the First World War. This also implied a tremendous military potential, the consciousness of which had its own effect on the conduct of foreign policy. Not only William II, but his Chancellors and generals and admirals, were aware of the power at their disposal. This, and the relative ease with which Germany sustained its massive war production in 1914-18, perhaps camouflaged the country's essential vulnerability in any two-front war, and made the eventual defeat in 1918 all the more traumatic.

A divided society?

The study of Wilhelmine social history is still relatively new.

Although in the last decade a number of valuable works have appeared (**88**; **99**; **120**; **122**; **91**), some German social historians have tended to see the period more in the light of theory than empirical historical investigation (**40**; **210**). Until recently German social history has also suffered from a lack of comparisons with other societies (**102**; **118**; **110**).

The increase in population, together with the migration of large numbers of people from one part of Germany to another, was one of the greatest strains on Wilhelmine society. Most of this increase flooded into the towns: whereas in 1890 47 per cent of Germans were city dwellers, by 1910 the figure was 60 per cent. In 1871 only eight German towns had more than 100,000 inhabitants; in 1910 there were forty-eight, accounting for 21.3 per cent of the population. Berlin's population doubled between 1875 and 1910; Munich's tripled; Essen and Kiel were six times as populous. There was a vast regional transfer of population, not only from country to town, but from east to west, as Germans left the land in their millions to seek work in the more industrialised areas. By 1907 the industrial Rhineland and Westphalia had together absorbed over a million people (**86**; **108**; **120**). To add to the problems spawned by this internal exodus, many of the migrants were not Germans but Poles or east European Jews; and in the eastern provinces the urban population became increasingly Polish (**82**; **39**; **95**; **103**; **127**).

For all the upheaval in ordinary people's lives which such change suggests, Wilhelmine society was still fairly rigidly divided along class lines. The pace of change after 1890 was unprecedented, but what little we know of class structures suggests that there was still relatively little social mobility (**120**). Perhaps, under the surface, far greater changes were taking place than people realised at the time. But to contemporary observers Wilhelmine society, to use a modern sociological term, remained 'pillarised', in the sense that an assortment of different, compartmentalised classes and groups all supported the state and monarchy, without having much else in common with one another (**69**). Landowners, industrialists, shopkeepers and workers; Protestants and Catholics; academics and bureaucrats, all pursued their own interests, only notionally united by the concept of a German nationality. In addition, regional traditions were still strong enough to remind the Prussian or Bavarian or Saxon that there were not only different classes but different Germans as well.

The nobility was still a powerful and numerous group. Nobles enjoyed an automatic preferment in appointments to the court, the army and the bureaucracy. Noble landowners also benefited, especially in Prussia, from relatively low taxation and special credit facilities. The result was a class which served as a bastion of conservative values, anti-democratic, anti-industrialist and paternalistic; and which not only ruthlessly defended its interest in high tariffs, but secured considerable support in doing so from the small farmers of north-west and south-west Germany (**64**; **76**; **109**). Whether it is correct, in view of the social, economic and political influence exercised by the nobility, to say that the middle classes absorbed their 'pre-industrial values', is still a matter for debate (**29**; **120**; **34**) [**doc. 11**].

The great industrialists, the Krupps, Thyssens and Hugenbergs, and the rest of the upper middle class, may be considered part of this same elite. Certainly the ostentation of their life-style [**doc. 12**], which in the late nineteenth century was 'an increasingly common feature of successful industrialists' (**120**, p. 210), set them apart from the rest of society. The industrialist of the Wilhelmine period was frequently happy to buy a landed estate and an army commission for his son, and to contribute to the right-wing parties. Industrialists could also be markedly patriarchical and authoritarian in their attitudes to their work-force [**doc. 13**], often demanding the greatest possible control over workers' lives, their free time, even their reading material (**30**; **120**). Most were not only uncritical of the existing system, but ready to identify with its values (**105**; **74**).

Two distinct castes in Wilhelmine society were bureaucrats and academics. Bureaucrats accounted for some 5 per cent of the population by 1907 and, especially in Prussia, were indeed 'a kind of semi-independent class' (**120**, p. 207). Their personal oath of loyalty to the monarch; the code of behaviour which governed their lives; their economic security, all fostered an *esprit de corps* in German officials, a sense of exclusivity, a social prestige (**119**). Academics, both university professors and schoolteachers, were also state employees. The respect accorded learning made them regard themselves as an elite, and they were more likely to be defenders of the status quo than critics of society. Academics were also strongly nationalist, and formed the backbone of pressure groups designed to promote *Weltpolitik* (**100**; **117**).

The lower middle class embraced a wide variety of occupations and standards of living. This was the class of small businessmen, shopkeepers, artisans, minor officials, small farmers and the new phenomenon of 'white collar' office employees. Although widespread, the lower middle class was particularly strong in the south, the centre and the north-west. Its livelihood was almost as much threatened by fluctuations in the economy as that of the working class. Unlike the majority of urban wage-earners, however, lower middle-class Germans were more receptive to critiques of industrialisation and modernity, and were apt to regard themselves as guardians of older, more 'moral' values. Artisans especially had been in decline throughout the century. They turned increasingly to right-wing pressure groups, including the anti-Semitic parties, as an outlet for their frustrations (**52**; **105**; **125**; **65**).

The lot of agricultural labourers and smallholders – the largest class in Germany until 1890, and even in 1914 some 15 per cent of the population – was particularly hard [**doc. 14a**]. Many had been reduced to dependency on seasonal labour, and the new breed of capitalist landowners, at least in east Prussia, was quite capable of slashing costs still further by importing cheaper labour, often Polish, from Russia and Austria-Hungary. Some smallholders did well, for example dairy and vegetable producers near the towns; or in Bavaria, where the law of primogeniture required them to pass on their holdings undiminished to their first-born. Elsewhere in Germany those peasants who owned their land tended to divide it among their children, which made subsistence even more difficult. Overpopulation drove living standards down still further, compelling more and more peasants to seek work in the cities. Like the urban artisans, those who remained saw industrialisation as their enemy: it was disaffected small farmers who provided the BdL with its mass following (**109**; **86**; **92**; **53**; **126**).

The urban working class was not much better off. Although real wages over the whole period rose, employers were still free to impose arbitrary wage cuts and sackings; and the value of the worker's pay-packet was further reduced by the high cost of basic foodstuffs. Hours gradually improved: between 1877 and 1912 the average working year was reduced from 3,300 hours to 2,970, the equivalent of about one day per week. The employment of women and children was subject to progressive restrictions, but the most crucial ingredient in such measures, rigorous inspection, was absent (**85**; **90**; **69**) [**doc. 14b**]. Housing was a major problem, with rents sometimes taking up to a fifth of a working-class family's income, and overcrowding and inadequate sanitation increasing the risk of disease. In Bochum in the Ruhr, for example, 84 per cent of the population were living with more than one person per room in 1905; cases were recorded of one-room dwellings with ten people or more living in them. Despite efforts to improve water supplies and sewage disposal, Bochum experienced a typhus outbreak as late as 1907; Hamburg was plagued by cholera epidemics regularly until shortly before the First World War. Industrial pollution was responsible for a far higher proportion of illnesses and deaths than it is today, especially respiratory diseases like tuberculosis and influenza (**99**; **88**; **122**; **91**).

Industrial workers have traditionally been seen as both socially cohesive and politically radical. Working-class solidarity was no doubt reinforced by the attitude of government and other social classes. In a society like Wilhelmine Germany, where leaders from William II downwards could persistently describe the existence of unions and a socialist party as a threat to the state, it is not surprising that workers felt a common identity, a sense of separateness that almost amounted to being in a working-class ghetto (**20**; **106**). But there has perhaps been too great a tendency to equate the history of the German working class with the history of the SPD. After 1890 there was a rapid growth of trade unionism, and it is true that most of these unions were led by Social Democrats. SPD trade unionists, however, were critical of the Party's revolutionary rhetoric; and the General Commission of Trade Unions, founded in 1890 by Carl Legien, was certainly not just an extension of the Party machine. Instead, by 1906 the General Commission had induced the SPD leadership to drop its policy of the political mass strike (**111**). Moreover, although the vast majority of industrial workers continued to vote SPD, and 85 per cent of trade unionists were affiliated to the General Commission, alternative non-socialist organisations did exist. Both Catholic and Protestant workers' clubs, specifically conceived as an antidote to the teachings of socialism, flourished even in the heavily industrialised Ruhr. In 1899, for instance, a largely Catholic Christian Trades Union Congress was held in Mainz; the movement had 341,000 members by 1913, or 11.4 per cent of total trades union membership (**85**; **120**).

Was Wilhelmine Germany, after almost half a century of political unity, a divided society? The answer must be a qualified 'yes'. There were two types of division. One was the class divide. To some extent this was the inevitable consequence of industrialisation, and in this Germany's experience was no different from that of other European societies. But in some respects the social divide was also an unnecessary creation of the ruling elite, which persisted in regarding the majority of German citizens, the working class, as beyond the pale. Given a different, more responsive set of political institutions, therefore, imperial Germany might with time have overcome its social divisions. Certainly the potential for real social strife, for violent revolution, was by 1914 almost non-existent in Germany; compare this with the situation in tsarist Russia, a social volcano, or in Britain, where the Irish problem was threatening civil war. The truly dangerous divisions in imperial Germany were not so much social as they were national. For Germany was not just composed of Germans; and in its treatment of minorities German society betrayed a nationalist aggression, with heavy racist undertones, which boded ill for the future.

The treatment of minorities

Imperial Germany, like Russia and Austria-Hungary, was a multinational empire. In 1910 the Polish, French and Danish minorities numbered 4,076,000 (**86**). Jews formed a special minority, whose treatment was a mix of religious, economic and racial prejudice. The existence of such minorities posed a problem, because the whole trend of nineteenth-century nationalism, with its emphasis on the need for cultural and linguistic unity, was inimical to their rights.

The very newness of their state led to anxiety among some Germans about its cohesion and territorial integrity. But for many others the new Empire was a source of national pride as much as anywhere else in Europe. The historian Heinrich von Treitschke personified this mainstream nationalism, and through his writings and lectures exerted an enormous influence on subsequent generations, including Bülow and Tirpitz. This sort of nationalism regarded minorities as a threat to national unity, but did not normally descend to racist exclusivity (**45**; **128**).

What has been called 'radical nationalism' (**47**, p. 40) was characteristic of those who were *not* satisfied with the existing state. The Pan-German League, for example, argued that Germany would never be truly unified until it included not only all Germans, but all peoples of 'Germanic' stock and, ideally, all territories which had been ruled by the old medieval German Empire. The Pan-Germans were firm advocates of a Greater Germany which would dominate Europe, and were noisily critical of the imperial government for not doing enough in this direction (**87**; **173**). The attitude of most radical nationalist organisations towards Germany's minorities was uncompromising: as non-Germans they could not be entitled to equal citizenship, and if they refused to assimilate, they ought to be expelled (**46**; **58**; **65**; **95**; **124**).

Neither assimilation nor expulsion proved practicable in the case of the Poles, at 5 per cent of the population Germany's largest minority (**39**). The 2.4 million Poles in Prussia found themselves subjected to a mounting drive to 'Germanise' them. A series of measures aimed at eliminating Polish from use in government, the courts and schools culminated in the Settlement Law of 1886. This made provision for a Settlement Commission to buy up estates from Polish landowners and colonise them with German peasants (**95**; **84**; **22**).

After a period of relaxation under Caprivi (**84**), this policy was carried on with renewed determination, but with indifferent results. Despite the acquisition of about half a million hectares (71 per cent of it from German, not Polish, landowners), and the settlement of 150,000 Germans in eastern Prussia, the German government found its own weapon turned against it. Polish nationalism was awakened in the peasantry and the growing middle class of the east Prussian towns. A largely middle-class party, the National-Democratic Association (*TDN**), arose and by the 1907 elections had twenty seats in the Reichstag. Poles organised their own cooperatives and lending societies for buying land themselves, with such success that between 1896 and 1914 more land was transferred from Germans to Poles than from Poles to Germans (**84**; **95**; **124**). This trend would probably have been even more pronounced, had not many Poles already migrated to the west of Germany in search of work: by 1914 there were about 400,000 Poles in the Ruhr alone (**39**; **103**).

The imperial government refused to admit defeat. The Germanisation of Polish schools was completed, in the face of mass 'school strikes' by Polish pupils, in the winter of 1906–07 (**104**). The Expropriation Law of 1908 attempted to solve the Settlement Commission's problems by making the sale of Polish estates compulsory, although there were doubts even in the Prussian *Landtag* about this violation of property rights. The Imperial Associations Law, in the same year, restricted the use of any language other than German at public meetings (**39**). By 1914 the government had not simply failed to integrate the Poles; it had given them all the more reason to hope for the resurrection of a Polish national state [**doc. 15**].

In Alsace-Lorraine the population, although overwhelmingly German-speaking, continued to think of themselves as French. In addition 80 per cent of them were Catholics. But in theory the obstacles to assimilation were not great. Annexation had been dictated more by considerations of military security than nationalism.

This led to a curious ambivalence in government policy. The civilian government wished to assimilate the population as 'Germans'; the military and the provincial administration reacted to the slightest show of disaffection with the denial of basic rights and petty restrictions. This only served to keep a sense of separateness alive (**121**; **39**; **69**) [**doc. 16**].

In Lorraine the government pursued a policy of Germanisation of the French-speaking minority, by progressively restricting the hours of instruction in French in the schools. A colonisation programme in both provinces was even considered, although this was only begun during the First World War. In fact demographic change was likely to be more effective than government action. Between 1871 and 1910 an estimated 460,000 Alsace-Lorrainers emigrated, mainly to France. At the same time the number of 'old Germans' (immigrants from the Reich) increased by 170,000. If the imperial government had been content to leave things alone, there was at least a possibility that with time Alsace-Lorrainers would have grown accustomed to being Germans. Instead, flare-ups like the notorious Zabern incident in 1913 continued to make German rule unpopular in Alsace-Lorraine and thoroughly ridiculous abroad. At Zabern, in Lower Alsace, a Prussian infantry lieutenant made himself so loathed by the locals that his colonel was reduced to providing him with an escort every time he entered the town; this produced further friction and demonstrations, at which the colonel and his men arbitrarily arrested twenty-seven citizens (**69**).

The Danish minority in northern Schleswig was also a legacy of Bismarck's wars. Over the years a majority of Danes appear to have resigned themselves to German citizenship. This did not make them willing subjects, nor did the imperial government regard them as such. Danes who 'opted' not to be German citizens were summarily deported; the use of Danish in state schools was suppressed; nationalist leaders were constantly harassed and even imprisoned [**doc. 17**]. A 'battle for the soil' similar to that in eastern Prussia was waged, with the government trying to settle Germans, and Danish self-help organisations resisting (**96**).

There was a difference between Germany's national minorities and its Jewish population, since most of the latter considered themselves German. Yet there was no denying that Jews formed a distinct group, though never more than 1 per cent of the population in the Wilhelmine period. Enduring prejudices ensured that some doors, such as the army, the senior bureaucracy and the judiciary, were still barred to them. The economic elite included some of the wealthiest men in the Reich: the banking families of Rothschild and Warburg; Albert Ballin the shipping magnate; the brilliant Rathenaus (**113**; **114**). Jews were prominent in the professions, too, as lawyers, doctors, scientists, teachers, artists, journalists (**120**). Then there was the broad mass of Jews who, contrary to the popular image, scraped a living as petty tradesmen and craftsmen. One group of Jews, however, remained painfully unintegrated. From the early 1880s, large numbers of east European Jews, driven out of tsarist Russia, began flooding into Germany. Some 79,000 by 1910, they were subjected to petty harassment and control by German officials, since they had no clear legal status. It was partly their presence which, during the First World War, helped spread anti-Semitism (**127**).

A pseudo-scientific racism was popularised by Ernst Haeckel, whose best-selling *The Riddle of the Universe* (1899) classified mankind into 'higher' and 'lower' races; the Germans, according to Haeckel, were a distinctly 'higher' people (**94**; **101**). Even more explicit warnings on race came from Julius Langbehn's equally popular *Rembrandt as Educator* (1890), which identified the Jews in particular as a 'poison' in German society which had to be exterminated (**123**). This idea of alien races as a biological threat to German racial 'purity' was furthered by Houston Stewart Chamberlain, an Englishman who made Germany his adopted home. His *The Foundations of the Nineteenth Century* (1899) equated the 'fitness' of a race with the extent to which it had preserved its essential character; allowing Jews to intermarry with Germans was to imperil the Germanic race. Chamberlain's book was read and admired by William II, and provided subsequent racists with many of their basic ideas (**93**).

It would be wrong, however, to regard anti-Semitism as merely the concern of intellectuals; attacks upon Jewish influence met with a ready response. By 1894 no fewer than seven different anti-Semitic parties had finally merged as the German Social Reform Party, a union which lasted until 1900 (**65**). The adoption of some elements of anti-Semitic propaganda by the Conservative Party in 1892 was an attempt to win the support of these voters. The Pan-Germans also spread anti-Semitic propaganda [**doc. 18**]. Comments like Treitschke's 'The Jews are our national misfortune' showed that such prejudice was socially acceptable (**20**, p. 154).

It took the pressures of the War to bring the particularly virulent form of anti-Semitism, which the Nazis exploited in the 1920s, out into the open. This was in spite of the obvious patriotism of German

Jews, who died in their thousands for the Reich and who, on the home front, made major contributions to the war effort. Other factors, however, bred prejudice. The marooning on German soil of large numbers of Russian Jews raised irrational fears of an 'eastern Jewish peril', and after 1916 anti-Semitic literature began to proliferate (**127**). The high profile of businessmen like Ballin and Walther Rathenau in running the war economy provoked cries of sabotage and Jewish conspiracy. By 1917, Pan-Germans in the high command were using statistics about the number of Jews in sensitive posts to incite popular suspicions still further. By 1918, some observers were already predicting that the Jews were being made scapegoats for Germany's defeat (**130**).

5 The Armed Forces

The army

It would not be too much of an exaggeration to say that the army in Wilhelmine Germany was a 'state within the state' (**132**, p. 217). Technically there was no such thing as a 'German' army, but rather the four armies of Prussia, Bavaria, Saxony and Württemberg. Because of its size, however, the Prussian army was the only one that mattered.

To avoid Reichstag interference, effective strength for the armies as a whole had been legally fixed since 1874 by the so-called 'iron budget'. This removed the army from annual budgetary control by committing the Reichstag to provide funds for a fixed period, after 1893, of five years (**5**; **132**).

The army's hierarchy was a continuation of absolutist traditions. The military cabinet advised the Emperor on appointments and promotions, which increased their influence enormously. The general staff, charged with planning, mobilisation and the direction of operations, also had direct access to the Emperor. This absence of effective civilian control over the military had disastrous consequences, because the army was free to advise the Emperor on political matters, both domestic and international. Its often irresponsible interventions helped bedevil the government's relations with both the Reichstag and neighbouring states, and strengthened the natural tendency of soldiers to think of their job in purely military terms, divorced from political reality. This had especially unfortunate results in the realm of war plans (**138**; **142**, vol. 2).

Strategy was dictated by the automatic hostility of France, because of Germany's annexation of Alsace-Lorraine, and after 1890 by the growing perception of the threat Russia posed both economically and militarily. The assumption therefore was of a war on two fronts, with Germany supported by its ally Austria-Hungary. Because of the greater time needed by Russia to mobilise, the general staff considered it imperative to strike first against France. The plan drawn up in 1905 by General Alfred von Schlieffen therefore envisaged outflanking French forces by means of a massive swing through Belgium; with France overwhelmed, the German army would contain a Russian onslaught in the east (**141**) [**doc. 19**].

It is probable that Germany never possessed adequate numbers of troops to ensure the effectiveness of the Plan. Even more seriously, Belgium's neutrality was guaranteed by international treaty, which meant that any violation of Belgian territory made Britain's involvement against Germany almost inevitable. This was the cardinal idiocy of the Schlieffen Plan. As even the conservative German historian Gerhard Ritter put it, the Plan was the 'worst of all the available options' (**141**, p. 95).

What made the Schlieffen Plan even worse was its mechanistic time-factor. In order to gain time in the race to smash France before Russia was mobilised, the general staff would be anxious to attack the French as soon as possible, however tenuous the pretext for doing so. Thus military considerations crowded out political ones, and such was the army's prestige that no Chancellor even questioned these priorities. In any case, the general staff was under no obligation to reveal its plans to anyone save the Emperor, with the result that, although Bethmann Hollweg in 1914 knew about the intended violation of Belgian neutrality, he apparently did not realise the tightness of the time-table. The German government's hands were tied; unlike other powers' mobilisation plans, 'German mobilisation inevitably meant war' (**184**, p. 84).

In view of the Schlieffen Plan's requirements for ever more troops, it is odd that the army held off pressing for major increases in manpower until the two Army Laws of 1912–13 (**134**). For twenty years its demands had been 'remarkably moderate' (**20**, p. 294). It has been argued that the principal reason for this restraint was social and political rather than military. Expansion would make the recruitment of more middle-class officers unavoidable, and the army leadership 'feared that an influx of "undesirable" elements would destroy the homogeneity of the officer corps' (**13**, p. 7). This in turn would make the army less reliable against the 'forces of revolution' (**40**).

Recent research, however, suggests that too much should not be made of domestic political arguments in explaining the army's size. Equally important was the purely practical consideration that the army was already too big to ensure adequate training for its intake: in other words, it was the military, rather than the social quality of the army which most concerned the war ministry. When the general staff and the war ministry finally did sink their differences and apply for the massive increases of 1912–13, they were influenced most of all by the threatening international situation [**doc. 20**]. By 1914, as a result of the two Army Laws, Germany's standing army of 2,398,000 confronted the Russians, with 3,420,000, and the French, with 1,867,000. Together with Austria-Hungary's army this was considered a large enough force to tip the balance in Germany's favour (**143**; **170**; **10**; **134**).

By some conservative elements, the army was conceived as having a second function, namely as an instrument of social control. In the absence of a national police force, the army was seen by the imperial government as a legitimate means of preserving public order. This meant breaking strikes, and rehearsing absurdly exaggerated preparations for dealing with an armed revolt, based on a general staff publication of 1907, *Fighting in Insurgent Towns* [**doc. 21**]. The army took this seriously, and was frequently called in by local authorities to protect factories and strike-breakers, despite the fact that demonstrations and strikes led by the SPD almost invariably passed off peacefully.

Despite this repressive potential the army continued to be one of the most popular of Wilhelmine institutions. More ominous was the army's share in the spread of what has been called 'social militarism' (**40**, p. 156). Mass conscription and sheer numbers meant that soldiers were highly visible in German society, and too many people were ready to accept military values [**doc. 22**]. This showed itself in the respect accorded anyone in uniform, which encouraged civilians from the Chancellor down to appear in their reserve officers' tunics. The military's special status was conceded by the Empire's top civilians, such as Bethmann Hollweg, who in the words of an adviser was 'profoundly convinced that the Prussian-German state lived and died by its army' (**69**, p. 127), and who during the War would have thought it 'presumptuous' to question the generals' judgment.

The respect accorded them, or occasionally the *lack* of respect, encouraged the military to behave with even greater arrogance and independence than their special status warranted. Here the classic example was the Zabern incident, which sprang from the belief that the army was above the law. In the words of the local commander, 'This is where jurisprudence ends' (**69**, p. 111). Zabern also illustrated the extent to which the civilian government, even if it did not share this attitude, was nonetheless prepared to endorse it in public, lest the army's all-important prestige be diminished [**doc. 23**]. At best, the public outcry over Zabern was evidence that militarism was not the universal fetish of the German people.

Tirpitz and the navy

The growth of the German battle fleet in the Wilhelmine period was one of the most startling military developments in the world before 1914. By the outbreak of the First World War the navy was the second largest after the British. Naval construction on this scale was an index of Germany's industrial might: the fact that it could be done was significant in itself. But the navy's most important effect was the unmistakable threat it posed to British naval predominance. By its obstinate persistence in naval construction Germany ensured its own isolation (**144**; **139**; **13**).

The campaign for a strong navy had deep economic, political and social roots. No country, it was argued, could become a truly world power without a navy. The 'historical economists', such as Gustav Schmoller and Werner Sombart, taught that German commercial growth could only be achieved by a process of struggle. The claim was also made that Germany's population explosion made the acquisition of overseas territory for settlement a matter of urgency. These ideas were enthusiastically taken up by numerous public figures and nationalist organisations in the 1880s and 1890s (**144**).

Agitation for a navy received additional impetus with the publication of *The Influence of Sea-Power upon History* (1890), by the American, Captain Mahan. Mahan claimed to show that command of the sea was the decisive factor in Britain's rise to world power. His book exerted a considerable influence on the public perception of naval power in Germany, where by 1894 William II confessed he was 'not reading but devouring Captain Mahan's book' (**8**, p. 299). William's part in the creation of the modern battle fleet was to be crucial, for without his personal commitment to the building programme which Tirpitz submitted to him in 1897, and his repeated refusal to contemplate its abandonment, it is doubtful whether the German fleet could have assumed its formidable proportions (**131**; **139**).

It was Tirpitz, however, who provided the real motive power behind German navalism. Tirpitz reached most of Mahan's conclusions regarding sea-power independently, and saw Germany as the naval power of the future. Just as important, German admirals in this period were becoming convinced of the need for a fixed naval law, not unlike the army's 'iron budget'. But only Tirpitz seemed to possess a clear-cut plan for getting a new building programme through the Reichstag. In fact Tirpitz's parliamentary skills were decisive, since he was acute enough to realise the importance of harnessing both Reichstag and public opinion to his designs (**131**).

The fundamental strategic premise of the fleet, which Tirpitz spelt out for the Emperor in mid-1897, was its anti-British purpose [**doc. 24**]. Tirpitz proposed that Germany must create a well-trained battle fleet at least two-thirds the size of Britain's. A fleet this size would be able to inflict so much damage on the Royal Navy that even if it were defeated the British 'risked' losing their supremacy at sea forever. However, until the German fleet had been built, it would be exposed to attack by Britain (**13**).

To reduce this 'danger zone' Tirpitz intended keeping the scale of his plans secret for as long as possible. The 1898 Navy Law stipulated that Germany should have nineteen battleships by the year 1905, and committed the Reichstag to voting the funds for replacements of each ship after twenty-five years. What Tirpitz did not make clear was that he was already planning a total of sixty capital ships by 1917, and that proposals for more ships were being worked out even before the Reichstag had passed the 1898 Law. The Law of 1900 raised the projected fleet to thirty-eight ships. The *Novelle*, or supplementary law, of 1908 set the replacement time at twenty years. As late as 1912 Tirpitz managed to obtain yet another *Novelle*, and with it a 50 per cent increase in the number of ships in active commission (**131**; **139**).

How did Tirpitz do it? Part of the answer lies in the fact that, with the passing of the 1898 Law, the Imperial Navy Office had already won half the battle. The Reichstag was committed by law to pay not only for each year's new keels, but for their eventual replacements as well, regardless of how big or how costly such replacements might be. These provisions, once passed, could not be altered. No one effectively challenged this literally ironclad budgetary rule; but to be fair no one could have guessed just how deep-laid Tirpitz's plans really were.

The real secrets of Tirpitz's success were the novelty of his methods and the receptivity of many Germans to the idea of a navy. One of his first acts was to set up a 'Section for News and General Parliamentary Affairs', whose task was to be, in Tirpitz's own words, the 'mobilisation of the masses'. In the run-up to the Reichstag debates on the 1898 Bill alone, this news bureau recruited the assistance of industrialists and chambers of commerce; enlisted the sympathies of the press and supplied it regularly with information; and published its own journal, *Nauticus* (**144**) [**doc. 25**]. The Pan-German League received its propaganda straight from the news bureau; and the Colonial Society distributed some 2000 copies of Mahan's book. Most crucial was the agitation of the Navy League, founded in 1898 with the backing of the steel magnate, Krupp. The Navy League proved a runaway success, eventually attaining a membership of over a million people, most of them from the middle classes (**131**; **13**; **46**; **133**).

The popularity of the navy makes it hard to take at face value the thesis that the whole thing was manipulative (**13**; **131**). It certainly did not serve to bolster the interests of a so-called armaments ring (**133**; **140**); and most of the arguments that the navy was part of 'social imperialism' boil down to a single letter by Tirpitz in 1895, where he mentioned the possibility that the appeal of a fleet might lessen that of Social Democracy (**22**). Instead, Tirpitz hoped this might be one of the welcome side-effects of a project whose primary purpose was always the strategic one of confronting British sea-power. In Steinberg's words, 'Tirpitz wanted to build battleships. He never wanted to build a "system-stabilizing fleet" nor would he have understood what it meant' (**145**, p. 203). To this might be added that a lot of other people in Wilhelmine Germany wanted Tirpitz to build battleships too.

In the end, however, the 'Tirpitz plan' went disastrously wrong. It was essential to the success of the programme that there be no dramatic changes in British naval policy, but in 1905–06 the British Admiralty committed itself to a revolutionary new battleship design. HMS *Dreadnought* made the battle fleets of all other powers obsolete overnight. Dreadnoughts were also vastly more expensive. Not only were all the gains Tirpitz had made against Britain's naval superiority since 1898 wiped out; but the increased costs, if Germany followed the British lead, would impose a terrible strain on the imperial treasury (**136**).

The decisive setback to Tirpitz's strategy was the gradual realisation by the British that German naval expansion was aimed against them. There had not been much perception of the German fleet as a threat in the beginning, since the numbers involved – nineteen battleships in 1898 – could not compare with the 62 Britain already possessed (**137**). It was not until the *Novelle* of 1908 that the German challenge became unmistakable. The British government decided to double the number of capital ships laid down in 1909; and their answer to the 1912 *Novelle* was the announcement that henceforward for every one battleship started by Germany, Britain would start two (**175**; **13**; **161**).

In this game of numbers Germany was bound to come out the loser since, with its double commitment to both a large army and navy, it was in a far worse position to meet its bills. The cost of the fleet accounted for 23.7 per cent of government spending by 1908, as opposed to 17.9 per cent in 1901; between 1905–06 and 1914 costs went up by 105 per cent, whereas the increase for Britain in the same period represented only 28 per cent (**139**; **135**). But worst of all, the naval arms race decisively altered Anglo-German relations, in that for the first time war between the two powers began to seem a distinct possibility (**160**).

Tirpitz has some claim to be considered the 'evil genius' of Wilhelmine Germany (**20**, p. 310), not only for pursuing naval building in such a way, but also for sabotaging all attempts to reach a compromise with the British. Bülow, and after him Bethmann Hollweg, belatedly recognised the crippling cost of the navy both financially and diplomatically [**doc. 26**]. But as long as Tirpitz retained the support of William II there could be no question of abandoning the programme. Moreover, even Bethmann Hollweg persisted in offering terms which were completely unrealistic: Germany would only limit its construction if Britain would undertake to remain neutral in any European conflict. In the circumstances, this was utopian; Tirpitz could rest easy (**174**).

In his obsession with battleships, Tirpitz deliberately neglected other types of technology, such as U-boats (**147**). Yet Germany came closest to winning the war against Britain through unrestricted submarine warfare, and not through open battle in the North Sea. The whole naval programme was an expensive failure.

6 Foreign and Colonial Policy, 1890–1914

The quest for world power status

By 1890 Germany was a world power, with colonies as far afield as West Africa and the South Pacific. Colonial territory alone, however, was not seen as sufficient to guarantee equal status with the existing world powers of Britain, Russia, France and the United States. Government policy therefore reflected the aspirations of many Germans towards an even greater role on the world stage. What Bülow first referred to in 1897 as *Weltpolitik** has been seen as a coherent drive for world power, and its importance to an understanding of the origins of the First World War seems indisputable (**201**; **152**; **40**; **13**). But as Woodruff Smith has pointed out, *Weltpolitik* has usually been discussed without distinguishing between the different forms it took. There was a fundamental tension between what can be called economic imperialism, and a type of imperialism peculiarly German – the drive for colonial settlement in Europe, or *Lebensraum** (**173**; **171**).

Economic imperialism was by far the more influential in the period 1890–1914, to the point where it was 'institutionalised' in government departments, and in the academic and journalistic world (**173**, p. 54). Economic imperialism took two main forms. There were those who believed in the necessity of colonies for economic expansion, both as sources of essential raw materials and of cheap (i.e. native) labour, and as a secure market for manufactured goods (**184**). Most economic imperialists, however, regarded colonies as essentially peripheral to *Weltpolitik*. For all economic imperialists *Weltpolitik* meant gaining control of the means whereby Germany's economy could continue to expand; but for the majority an informal imperialism was sufficient. German products needed markets in more developed economies, such as the Americas and China, than the German colonial empire could provide. German capital sought large-scale investments simply not available in South West Africa or Samoa. To informal imperialists *Weltpolitik* came to

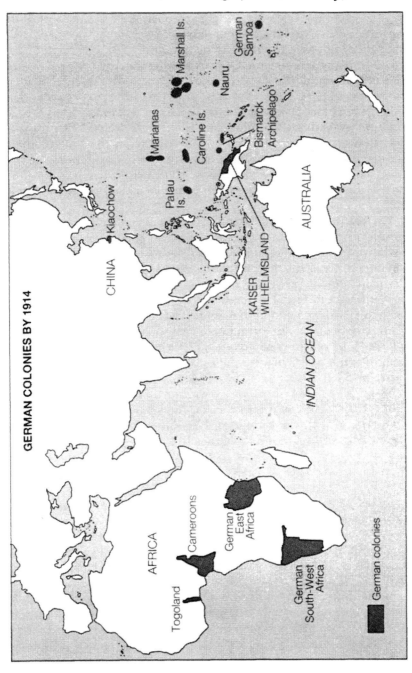

GERMAN COLONIES BY 1914

CHINA

Kiaochow

Marianas

Palau Is.

Marshall Is.

Caroline Is.

Nauru

German Samoa

Bismarck Archipelago

KAISER WILHELMSLAND

AUSTRALIA

INDIAN OCEAN

AFRICA

Togoland

Cameroons

German East Africa

German South-West Africa

German colonies

mean a foreign policy which promoted German commerce and industry abroad as forcefully as possible (**173**).

The second ideology, which demanded colonial settlement, was a
very different phenomenon. Distinctly anti-modernist, with a strong
racist emphasis on the importance of 'Germanness', its influence on
government policy until 1914 was much less than that of economic
imperialism. The term *Lebensraum* expresses accurately what settlement imperialists in the Wilhelmine era were after (**172**). One of
the strongest elements of support for the acquisition of colonies,
under Bismarck, was the enthusiasm of declining elements in the
lower middle class, who saw colonies as an opportunity for emigration and a new start in a more favourable economic climate (**125**;
52).

The idea of settlement also received a boost from the agrarian
movement. Emigration seemed to offer the possibility of relocating
peasants, made surplus by the capitalisation of German agriculture,
without threatening the interests of landowners. The colonies
Germany already possessed, however, proved unsuitable for extensive settlement. This led to calls for an expansion of Germany's
colonial territory, by force if need be (**64**; **87**; **112**).

Most ominous for the future was the growing demand for *inner*
colonisation, or the resettlement of Germans in the east of the
country. First advocated by the economist Max Sering and the influential Society for the Advancement of Inner Colonisation,
founded in 1893 (**41**), this policy was pursued by the government's
Settlement Commission and the Expropriation Law of 1908. Well
before the War it was being translated in some circles, notably the
Pan-German League, into an interest in territorial annexations in
eastern Europe (**87**). It was to bear bitter fruit in the Treaty of
Brest-Litovsk in 1918.

When one looks at the personalities who espoused these differing
forms of imperialism, the difficulty of regarding *Weltpolitik* as characteristic of Wilhelmine policy as a whole becomes apparent. The
majority voice, economic imperialism, undoubtedly found strong
support in the imperial chancellery, the foreign office and its off-
shoot, the colonial office, and in the world of big business (**173**;
201).

At the pinnacle of power, it becomes harder to be so categorical.
Both Bülow and Tirpitz talked the language of *Weltpolitik* [**doc. 27**],
but to a large extent this was window-dressing: it helped them
smooth over domestic political obstacles to their policies. Bülow's

outlook on the world in particular seems to have been shaped largely by a traditional diplomat's belief in the efficacy of power in international politics (**179**). Bethmann Hollweg, however, appears a more genuine convert to a *Weltpolitik* which included new colonies, or at least economic sway over central Africa and the Near East (**185**). The vagueness of *Weltpolitik* was epitomised by William II, who was by turn economic imperialist and *Lebensraum* enthusiast (**173**; **11**).

Elsewhere there was simply no consensus as to what Germany's role in the world should be. Academics, journalists and special-interest groups reflected all three types of imperialist thinking. Some public figures attempted a synthesis of the two rival strands of imperialism, but without notable success (**165**; **83**; **173**) [**doc. 28**]. At a popular level the preference seemed to be for a crude variety of *Lebensraum* imperialism. The Pan-German League was clearly and noisily in favour of an aggressive foreign policy, bigger and better colonies and inner colonisation. The Navy League was by definition in favour of *Weltpolitik* and colonies. There was a 'Society for Germandom Abroad', with 57,000 members by 1914; and the HKT Society, for Germandom at home, with 54,000 (**46**). Even the German Colonial Society, founded in 1887, was chronically riven by conflicts between settlement and economic colonialists (**171**; **167**).

What did this debate over Germany's imperialist mission amount to, in terms of practical results? As far as the German colonial empire is concerned, not very much. Germany's colonies by 1890 consisted of four large African possessions: South-West Africa, Togoland, the Cameroons, and East Africa (Tanzania); and, in the Pacific, 'Kaiser Wilhelmsland' (north-eastern New Guinea), the Bismarck Archipelago, Palau and the Marshall Islands. Heligoland in the North Sea was acquired from Britain in 1890, in return for the island of Zanzibar. To this were added the Chinese treaty port of Kiaochow in 1897 and, in the Pacific, part of Samoa and the Caroline and Mariana Islands in 1899. The Morocco crisis of 1911 won Germany a strip of the French Congo (**171**).

The truth was that Germany's colonies were less than profitable. The discovery of diamonds in South-West Africa in 1908, for instance, did not cover the costs of administration there, particularly since the colonial government had already had to put down the native Herero and Nama uprisings in 1904–07 (**148**; **149**). None of the other colonies offered even as much economic potential, with the possible exception of Kiaochow, the acquisition of which was supposed to facilitate informal economic imperialism in China (**158**; **166**). The fact that German business was in general unwilling to invest in the colonies was tacit acknowledgement of their practical worthlessness. They were not even attractive for settlement colonisation, however much the diehard proponents of *Lebensraum* denied this (**171**; **173**).

More rewarding were attempts at informal imperialism. This took the form of extensive investments in and trade with Latin America, China and in particular the countries of south-eastern Europe and the Middle East. Here, if anywhere, the close cooperation of government and business which the Fischer school have claimed was the hallmark of *Weltpolitik* can be seen in action. The great banks and the foreign office worked hand in hand to realise the Baghdad railway project, which held out the prospect of German access to the Middle Eastern oil fields (**153**; **80**), and agreements were signed with Turkey for the training of the Turkish army by Prussian officers (**227**). German trade treaties took advantage of Austria-Hungary's bad relations with the Balkan states, and German finance and manufactured goods flowed into the Balkan economies (**154**; **163**). The industrialist Hugo Stinnes may have exaggerated in 1911 when he told the Pan-German leader, Heinrich Class, that another three or four years of peace would make Germany 'undisputed master of Europe' [**doc. 29**], but the essential insight was correct: informal imperialism was more profitable than colonialism.

The ultimate political costs of German imperialism were huge. To the extent that it sustained Tirpitz's battle fleet, the resulting antagonism with Britain can be said to have been *Weltpolitik*'s most fateful contribution to Germany's growing isolation (**160**). Almost as dangerous was *Weltpolitik*'s most 'successful' aspect, its penetration of the Near and Middle East. This conjured up a strategic threat to Russia, a large proportion of whose grain exports passed through the Straits, and which regarded Germany's steady advances in the economic and military control of Turkey with alarm (**153**; **188**; **156**). *Weltpolitik* was thus involving Germany in fundamental differences with its two most formidable neighbours. Finally, pursuit of world-power status produced its own boomerang effect, in that German public opinion, conditioned by two decades of rhetoric about Germany's need for colonies, about its cultural mission in the world, came to expect more than the government could possibly deliver.

The failure of German diplomacy, 1890–1914

The process by which imperial Germany went from the apparent security of the Bismarckian system of alliances, in 1890, to the gamble of 1914, can be summarised as follows. Germany's position underwent two major deteriorations after Bismarck's fall. The first saw the lapse of treaty links between Germany and Russia and the consequent swing by the Russians towards an alliance with France, and was in a sense unavoidable (**156**). For the second, the estrangement of Britain and its gradual re-alignment with the Franco-Russian alliance between 1898 and 1907, the German government had mainly itself to blame. By 1907 the division of Europe into two hostile blocs of powers, the Dual Alliance of Germany and Austria-Hungary and the Triple Entente of France, Russia and Britain, was complete (**160; 175; 188**). German diplomacy from here on was characterised by a growing sense of encirclement and a strong desire to do something about it. Despite a continuing debate as to whether the Bethmann Hollweg government, after 1912, was determined to *provoke* a war, the evidence to date suggests that this was not the case. Instead, some German leaders, among them the Chancellor, regarded Germany's position more and more pessimistically, to the point where war began to seem an option almost imposed upon Germany; while others, especially the military, were confident Germany could break its ring of enemies by conducting a preventive war, as long as it acted soon enough. The argument was only resolved by the decision to *risk* war in 1914 (**189**).

Diplomacy under William II reflected the personality of the monarch, in its often transparent duplicity, its tendency to bluster first and then back down, the inordinate fuss it raised about relatively unimportant issues, and the inflated claims it made on behalf of Germany's role in Europe and the world. The very vagueness of German diplomacy led to confusion and suspicion in other European capitals.

When Caprivi took over from Bismarck he was quick to realise the tension between Germany's alliance with Austria-Hungary and its Reinsurance Treaty with Russia. In March 1890, the Treaty was allowed to lapse, a decision which was part of a general cooling in Russo-German relations already under way. The economic rivalry between the two countries, in particular the threat Russian grain posed to agrarian prosperity, was becoming obvious. By 1890 growing nationalism on both sides made purely dynastic links seem irrelevant. Nevertheless the Russian government took the lapse of the Treaty as proof of German hostility. By the time of the Franco-Russian Alliance of 1894, relations between Russia and Germany had sunk to an all-time low (**62**; **156**).

It was under Bülow that the second stage in Germany's diplomatic isolation was completed. Bülow's concept of *Weltpolitik* was grounded in the belief that a global conflict between Britain and Russia was inevitable. He was inclined to side with the Russians, although only once they were clearly winning. Moreover, if Germany could tilt the balance with a fleet large enough to challenge the Royal Navy, it could then supplant Britain as the leading world power (**178**). This was the so-called policy of the 'free hand'. All Germany had to do was 'to preserve good relations with both Britain and Russia and, in the possession of a strong fleet, to await calmly the future development of elemental events' (**20**, p. 311).

The Navy Laws of 1898 and 1900 made Germany's determination to establish itself as a serious naval power unmistakable. German popular hostility to Britain during the Boer War was deliberately fanned by Bülow in his speeches and through articles inspired by the foreign office's press bureau (**178**; **160**). The British reaction, however, when it came, was the very last thing Bülow had expected. Faced with the improbability of improving relations with Germany except on prohibitive terms, Britain gradually resolved its differences with its other main rivals, France and Russia. The first reconciliation was the *Entente Cordiale* of 1904 with France (**175**).

The German reaction to the Entente was typical: Bülow erroneously took it to be directed against Germany. In March 1905 the Emperor was persuaded to land in Morocco, where the French were planning to extend their colonial empire, and to make provocative noises about Germany's right to be consulted. The real motive was to split the Entente; but Bülow's policy from first to last was one of bluff (**168**; **185**). By forcing the resignation of the anti-German French foreign minister, Delcassé, the German government created a real fear of war. They then made things worse by demanding an international conference on the question. At the Conference of Algeciras in January 1906, however, they found themselves outvoted and obliged to accept a French protectorate in Morocco. The net result was to drive Britain and France even closer, since in reaction to the war-scare they began military consultations which were to continue down to 1914, transforming the Entente into a tacit alliance (**175**).

The belligerence of German diplomacy had an even more calamitous effect: it facilitated an understanding between Britain and Russia. Both were annoyed at the patent attempts by the German government to sow discord between them during the Russo-Japanese War (1904–05). Now they began to see advantages in patching up their differences; and in 1907 a somewhat shaky agreement was reached. This Triple Entente closed the circle: France, Russia and Britain were all now leagued against Germany and Austria-Hungary. Bülow's foreign policy lay in ruins.

The Triple Entente, though an understandable reaction to the blundering offensiveness of German policy, provoked a nearly hysterical response [**doc. 30**]. The conviction gained ground that Germany was being deliberately 'encircled', and German leaders began to set renewed store by their only ally, the Habsburg Monarchy. Consequently, when Austria-Hungary's annexation of the Turkish provinces of Bosnia-Hercegovina in 1908 led to a confrontation with Serbia and, behind the Serbs, Russia, Bülow decided to support the Austrians in the most tactless possible way. The Russian government in March 1909 was presented with a virtual ultimatum, forcing it to accept the annexation, but this poisoned relations still further (**188**).

When Bethmann Hollweg took over in June 1909, he brought to his office a less abrasive diplomatic style, as well as a greater sense of urgency regarding the need for better relations with Germany's potential enemies. Yet Bethmann Hollweg also had his own vision of *Weltpolitik* [**doc. 31**]. This became clear in the second Moroccan crisis of 1911. Here the goal, the extension of German influence in Central Africa, was limited, but the means employed was deliberately provocative. France and Britain were at first convinced the Germans were threatening war; and although in the end the French were glad to be able to buy Germany off with a slice of the French Congo, the uncertainty as to German intentions was only heightened (**55**; **153**; **185**).

In Germany there was widespread disappointment that the 1911 crisis had produced so little concrete gain. However, the view that Germany conducted a 'retreat to the European continent' after 1911, because *Weltpolitik* had 'failed', seems an exaggeration (**13**). On the contrary, Bethmann Hollweg was as determined as ever to create a space for Germany in the outside world, but he had to take account of increasingly unpleasant realities. One was the sudden breakdown of stability in south-eastern Europe. As a result of the Balkan Wars of 1912–13, Austria-Hungary now faced the possibility of attack by the Balkan states, especially Serbia. The sense of being encircled could only be increased by these events.

Germany's vulnerability was underlined in December 1912, when the British government felt obliged to warn Berlin that in the event of a European war it was unlikely that Britain would remain on the sidelines. In reaction, William II melodramatically called a 'war council' on 8 December 1912 (**153**; **169**). The German government did not at this point, however, or at any other, start conspiring to provoke a war (**189**). The main practical upshot of the 'war council' was the decision to expand the army even further in 1913 (**143**).

By mid-1914 Germany's situation had not changed dramatically since the close of the Balkan Wars. The government continued to support economic expansion in the Balkans and the Ottoman Empire. There was a limited improvement in relations with Britain over colonial matters, but Bethmann Hollweg found other developments less encouraging. News had reached the German government of talks between Britain and Russia regarding a possible naval convention. However untenable the suggestions that this forced Bethmann Hollweg to envisage a preventive war (**191**; **181**), the Chancellor was undoubtedly concerned. He was even more oppressed by the projected increase in Russian power [**doc. 33**]. Too much has perhaps been made of this 'cultural pessimism' as an explanation of German policy in 1914. Certainly the army was ready for a conflict, and it was likely that Bethmann Hollweg was influenced by their confidence (**189**). It is more accurate to say that the German government by 1914 was looking for a chance to break out of encirclement, confident of its strength and determined to seize on the first suitable pretext for demonstrating this.

The miscalculated risk of 1914

There have been four main interpretive trends discernible in the controversy over the origins of the war. Fischer's contribution was to make it impossible convincingly to deny the German government's essential responsibility. But his thesis, that Germany in 1914 deliberately unleashed a war for continental and even world hegemony, has never been universally accepted. Nor did the radicalisation of Fischer's claims make things easier: in his *War of Illusions* (1969) he attempted to show that, from the 'war council' of December 1912, the German government was consciously working towards a European war for the furtherance of expansion on the Continent (**153**; **73**; **3**; **177**).

A second interpretation revolves around the idea of 'preventive defence', the argument that the Bethmann Hollweg government deliberately provoked a diplomatic crisis which it knew might lead to war, but that this was because of deep-rooted and understandable concern at Germany's isolation, and fears of growing Russian strength (**191**). Central to this thesis are two arguments. One is that the news of the Anglo-Russian naval talks had a decisive effect in shaping Bethmann Hollweg's strategy (**191**; **1**; **187**). The other is that civilian and military leaders were much influenced by a deep pessimism as to Germany's chances of survival, if it did not act before it was too late (**38**; **55**; **157**; **183**). The essentially preventive nature of the decision for war is also stressed by the theory of the 'escape forwards', the desire of the conservative elites to resolve their domestic difficulties by a nationally unifying war (**40**; **13**).

Recently, however, there has been something of a backlash against the idea of Germany's primary responsibility for the war. The complaint of German publicists in the 1920s, that Britain could have prevented hostilities had it 'at an early date made perfectly clear what attitude it would adopt in the case of war', has been revived (**181**, p. 368). Similar prominence has also been given to the old textbook view that all nations were collectively responsible for war, and to the argument that Germany's geographical position made its actions in 1914 essentially defensive (**187**; **36**; **176**).

An emerging fourth interpretation upholds German responsibility, but rejects the more radical of Fischer's claims, as well as the suggestion that the decision to risk war in 1914 was in any real sense defensive. Kaiser and Pogge von Strandmann see a consistent expansionism in German policy before 1914, which lay at the heart of Bethmann Hollweg's conduct during the July Crisis (**185**; **189**). This does not mean that the German government planned war, but rather that it considered war an acceptable option, mainly because it held a short war to be both probable and winnable. Once resolved to exploit the July Crisis, it did so not pessimistically but in a mood of belligerent optimism [**doc. 34**].

The July Crisis bears out this latter interpretation more than any other. Bethmann Hollweg was convinced of Germany's need to expand, although he may have been inclined to place less emphasis on colonial gains and to concentrate instead on the Near and Middle East and the formation of a central European economic union (**215**;

185; **189**). He still saw agreement with Britain as an essential precondition for expansion. He was also obsessed by the growth of Russia (**191**). At the core of his actions in July 1914 appears to have been a naïve belief that, by picking a quarrel with Russia which did not involve British interests, he could diminish the continental threat to Germany without incurring British hostility (**185**). In succumbing to this way of thinking, however, Bethmann Hollweg was ignoring his own experience since becoming Chancellor [**doc. 32**].

The immediate significance of the assassination of the Austrian Archduke Francis Ferdinand at Sarajevo, on 28 June 1914, was that it decided the leaders of Austria-Hungary on taking military action against Serbia. For this German backing was essential, since there was a strong probability that Russia would intervene on Serbia's behalf. The Germans gave their support for reasons which had very little to do with the rights and wrongs of Austro-Serbian antagonism. Bethmann Hollweg saw Sarajevo as a unique opportunity for challenging the Entente, since only by basing his diplomatic offensive on a question closely involving Austria-Hungary could Germany be sure of its cooperation (**182**; **55**) [**doc. 33**]. In this sense Sarajevo was an occasion, not a cause.

The Austro-Hungarian government intended to present an ultimatum to Serbia which was deliberately designed to be unacceptable, and the German government not only knew this but fully approved it. Both governments were aware that 'action against Serbia can lead to world war' [**doc. 33**]. The first stage of the July Crisis was thus from 28 June to 23 July, in which Berlin and Vienna agreed upon the need for a confrontation, and the Austrians settled down to draft their ultimatum. The extent of the collusion between the two governments was kept a close secret. Initial apprehensions of the Entente powers as to the possible consequences of Sarajevo were partially allayed; and an early warning by the British Foreign Secretary, Sir Edward Grey, that strong action against Serbia might have a disastrous effect on Russian opinion, was ignored by Berlin (**3**).

In the second stage, 23–28 July, the Austro-Hungarian ultimatum burst on the scene with devastating effect. There was immediate realisation by the Entente powers that Austria-Hungary was intent on forcing a showdown with Serbia; what was not at first appreciated was that the German government fully supported this. As a result the repeated offers of mediation made by Grey, which were communicated to Vienna *via* Berlin, had no effect, especially since the German government secretly made it clear to the Austrians that it expected the proposals to be rejected. In fact, the Germans were desperately anxious for the Austrians to act more quickly, precisely to forestall efforts at mediation. After the Serbian rejection of its ultimatum on 25 July, Austria-Hungary immediately broke off relations and, despite mounting indications that the Russians were prepared to fight, declared war on Serbia on the 28th. The next day, as if to underline their aggressive intentions, Austro-Hungarian forces bombarded Belgrade from across the Danube.

The uncertainty as to how far the Austrians meant to go ushered in the final phase, by pushing the Russian government into mobilisation. Despite considerable confusion in St Petersburg as to whether the Tsar should order partial or general mobilisation, the effect on the German government was bound to be the same: even the preliminary moves towards mobilisation in Russia meant that the German army would lose valuable time in implementing the Schlieffen Plan. And German mobilisation, unlike any other European power's, meant war, since the first steps were linked to the violation of Belgian neutrality (**146; 184**). But for Bethmann Hollweg the Russian move was precisely what he wanted, a chance to present any resulting conflict to the German people as a 'defensive' reaction to a Russian threat. He therefore told the Russians on the 29th that 'further continuation of Russian mobilisation measures would compel us to mobilise' (**3**, p. 285).

The same day the Chancellor made a clumsy but revealing overture to the British ambassador, which showed how much his mind was still running along lines laid down by *Weltpolitik*. Virtually admitting the German intention of not only attacking France but doing so *via* Belgium, Bethmann Hollweg bid for Britain's neutrality by assuring the ambassador that French territorial integrity would be respected, except with regard to colonies. The same applied to Belgium, if the Belgians did not resist. The British response, however, was an unequivocal indication that Britain would support France. Bethmann Hollweg's hope of keeping Britain out had crumbled. Once the news of Russia's final decision to order general mobilisation reached Berlin, Bethmann Hollweg no longer seriously thought of averting war. The race to mobilise was on, and in rapid succession the German government declared war on Russia on 1 August; invaded Luxembourg and presented an ultimatum to Belgium on 2 August; declared war on France on 3 August; and invaded Belgium the next day. The British declaration of war on Germany, also on the 4th, was by then a foregone conclusion.

It is difficult, in the light of the German government's

determination to force a crisis, to see the Entente powers' reactions as anything but defensive. Russia was certainly influenced by a fear of losing prestige and influence in the Balkans, as well as by nationalist pressure to act in defence of Serbia. Equally powerful, however, was the strategic fear of seeing the Balkans, the Straits and Asia Minor dominated by a hostile power bloc (**188**). The French were unlikely to stand by while Germany defeated their only Continental ally, and in any case were gratuitously attacked in accordance with the Schlieffen Plan (**186**). The British government's principal reason for supporting France was the traditional fear of seeing the Continent dominated by a strong military (and naval) power, although the invasion of Belgium had the added bonus of making the war against Germany a popular moral one (**175**).

The German government's intentions in July 1914 seem plain. It hoped to end its 'encirclement' by splitting the Entente over a Balkan issue, but if that failed, it was prepared to accept the risk of a two-front war and even the involvement of Britain. In doing so, Bethmann Hollweg had some hopes of continuing the expansion associated with *Weltpolitik*. He was *not* motivated by a desire to obliterate domestic unrest by embroiling the nation in a war; on the contrary, his one domestic political concern was to present the war to the SPD in such a way as to be sure of their support (**13**; **55**). Such a policy seems all the more aggressive in view of the fact that, militarily, Germany's position was not all that bad; the army believed it could still win a war, and this appears to have had its effect on Bethmann Hollweg's calculations. The July Crisis could be described as an exercise in brinkmanship that failed, a miscalculated risk; but neither civilian nor army leaders showed much hesitation in accepting that risk.

7 The Test of War, 1914–18

Domestic politics and the supremacy of the General Staff

The First World War is crucial to an understanding not only of how imperial Germany ended, but also of subsequent developments under the Weimar Republic, particularly the rise of Nazism and Communism. This was because the War produced a sort of political 'greenhouse effect', in that it forced the growth of certain trends evident, but not necessarily predominant, before 1914; it created a number of new social problems; and it left the German people traumatised and embittered by an unexpected defeat.

The War to begin with was highly popular, since most German people were sincerely convinced that Germany had been unjustly attacked. This explains the ready response in August 1914 to the Emperor's declaration that 'I no longer recognise parties; I recognise only Germans' (**20**, p. 340), and the acceptance by the parties of the *Burgfriede* or political truce. The most remarkable thing about the *Burgfriede* was the participation of the SPD, which voted unanimously in favour of war credits, thus giving the lie to forty years of propaganda about the unpatriotic nature of socialism (**216**).

The *Burgfriede* lasted well into the third year of the War. Although the initial euphoria was dissipated by the unexpected duration of hostilities, and the horrifying casualties caused increasing dissent within the parties, there was virtually no public criticism of the government until the Reichstag's Peace Resolution of July 1917. Even the SPD, until then, tended to regard such public wrangling as a danger to morale (**216; 218; 219**).

This political vacuum, and the influence which the military came to exert on policy, were direct results of the failure to win a speedy victory. By September 1914 the Schlieffen Plan had broken down. French and British resistance was more stubborn than anticipated, and the German offensive ground to a halt in the bloody attrition of trench warfare (**197**). In the East, despite striking successes against the Russians, there was similar stalemate (**224**). The conclusion of an alliance with Turkey on 2 August 1914, and the latter's entry into the War in November, provided some strategic relief by diverting Allied troops to the Middle East and the Straits, and by choking off Russia's economic lifeline to the Mediterranean (**227**). But this was offset by the entry of Italy into the War on the side of the Allies in May 1915 (**180**); and the general picture was a grim one. Germany's leaders had not reckoned with a long war, and the economy was not geared to the special requirements of war production.

By the autumn of 1914 stocks of munitions were virtually exhausted, while supplies of essential raw materials were also running low. At the suggestion of the industrialist Rathenau, a War Raw Materials Office (*KRA**) was set up within the Prussian War Ministry in August 1914. The KRA played a decisive role in organising a war economy. It created a national network of 'corporations', private companies which on behalf of the government bought, stored and distributed raw materials. Once established, the principle of government intervention represented by the KRA proliferated in all directions. It was especially important in solving the shortage of nitrates, which were essential for ammunition production. The discovery of an artificial process for making nitrates was immediately seized upon by the KRA and massively subsidised (**199**).

Labour policy during the War was similarly wide-reaching. Because of the shortage of manpower, a department in the War Ministry decided which workers must be exempted from military service, and in which industries. In an attempt to minimise industrial unrest, the government recommended the setting up of local 'War Boards', on which representatives of management and workers were expected to arbitrate disputes. This development, unthinkable before the War, gave workers in the war industries a greater say and increased wages. It also created grave social tensions, since these workers seemed to be doing excessively well out of the War, compared to other industries, farmers and the middle class (**199; 210; 217**).

In two areas, however, government direction of the war economy proved wanting. The financing of the war effort reflected all the shortcomings of the federal constitution, since no national income tax was ever agreed upon. Worse, no ceiling was imposed on the profits made by industry out of war production, nor were such profits even taxed before 1916. The imperial German government could only cover 16 per cent of its expenditure through taxation (**40**). Instead, Germany floated through the War, on a sea of paper money. On the assumption that Germany would collect reparations from its enemies after the War, the treasury repeatedly increased the supply of banknotes, and covered the rest of expenditure by a massive sale of war-bonds [**doc. 35**]. This not only saddled the government with a huge national debt, but also created the inflation which was to contribute so much to the instability of the Weimar Republic (**80**; **200**; **213**).

More serious was the inability to do anything about the food shortages imposed by the Allied blockade. Germany in 1913 imported one-third of its foodstuffs, and the shortfall caused by the blockade was compounded by labour shortages on the land once the male population was mobilised; the yield of the 1917 harvest in essential cereals, for instance, was only half that of 1913 (**40**). Government intervention was belated and not particularly effective, partly because of the resistance offered by landowners to any control of their profits, partly because of the difficulties of requisitioning crops from small farmers who themselves had little enough to survive on (**199**). The result was a rise in prices and a flourishing black market. By the winter of 1916–17 there was widespread starvation, from which, on a conservative estimate, some 700,000 people were to die before the War ended (**40**; **193**; **228**) [**doc. 40a**]. This increased the pressure on the government to resort to unrestricted submarine warfare, as a means of forcing Britain out of the War and lifting the blockade.

The remarkable thing about the war economy in Germany, in contrast to the other major powers, was the extent to which it was controlled by the military. The KRA, the raw materials corporations, the War Boards, were all subordinate to the War Ministry, and most of the personnel involved were army officers. A base was thus created which enabled the Army Supreme Command (*OHL**) to project itself further and further into political matters.

Until the end of 1915 Bethmann Hollweg received more support than interference from General Erich von Falkenhayn, chief of the general staff, in resisting the demands of Tirpitz for unrestricted submarine warfare. Bethmann Hollweg knew this would almost certainly bring the United States into the War in protest against the sinking of American merchant vessels. Tirpitz was forced to resign in March 1916. By that time, however, Falkenhayn had changed his mind: determined to launch a major offensive at Verdun, he now felt unrestricted submarine warfare was the only hope of weakening the Allies sufficiently to ensure success (**207**; **136**).

Falkenhayn's conversion, and the appalling losses of 1916, decided Bethmann Hollweg on his replacement in August. In this the Chancellor was supported for purely opportunistic reasons by the team responsible for Germany's eastern successes, Field Marshal Paul von Hindenburg and his second in command, Erich Ludendorff, who thus assumed joint direction of the OHL. Hindenburg and Ludendorff enjoyed a tremendous popularity which, as they were only too aware, gave them a leverage Bethmann Hollweg could not ignore. They were also much more politically minded than Falkenhayn, being not only reactionary conservatives but also proponents of a ruthless prosecution of the War, extreme territorial annexations, and, as it happened, unrestricted submarine warfare. For both, the interests of the army and the war effort took priority over everything else, and in pursuit of this narrow vision they arrogated to the OHL a greater and greater share in the decision-making process of the Reich (**205**; **132**). Some of the devoted staff-officers on whom they relied were openly advocating a military dictatorship before the end of 1916 (**208**); but Hindenburg and Ludendorff favoured a 'silent dictatorship', whereby the army could control government policy without being seen to do so (**209**).

The emergence of the Hindenburg-Ludendorff team constituted 'a kind of political revolution' (**20**, p. 377), since the generals justified every intervention in government on grounds of overriding military necessity. Thus they sabotaged several openings for a negotiated peace. A possible opportunity in late 1916 to treat separately with the Russians, for instance, was blasted by the OHL's insistence on the proclamation of an 'independent' Poland. The army's reason was the chance this would offer of raising several divisions of Polish volunteers for Germany. That the proclamation made it politically impossible for the Russian government to pursue a separate peace was a matter of indifference to Hindenburg and Ludendorff (**194**). And Bethmann Hollweg's December 1916 note to President Wilson, setting out Germany's conditions for peace, was emasculated before it ever left Berlin by OHL demands for a close link with Belgium after the War, including possession of Liège and German control of Belgian railways (**201**; **198**) [**doc. 39**].

Military influence did not stop there. The generals demanded, and got, the dismissal of officials and even ministers, like the Foreign Secretary Jagow in November 1916, for insufficient 'toughness' in prosecuting the War. More fundamental was the Auxiliary Service Law of December 1916, which amounted to 'a complete militarisation of society' (**40**, p. 206). All males from seventeen to sixty were liable to compulsory labour service, and the War Ministry could direct them to work in particular areas of industry. Permission was required to change one's place of work, and employers could not take on workers without proof that they had such permission. Fierce penalties were prescribed for breaking these rules. But the Auxiliary Service Law could not stem a rising tide of disputes and strikes. Food shortages and the black market made workers increasingly desperate in pressing their claims, and their impatience was exacerbated by the vast profits which industry continued to make out of the War (**210**; **199**).

The final impetus towards effective military control of the German government was provided by the conflict between Bethmann Hollweg and the OHL over unrestricted submarine warfare. The army was assiduous in cultivating political party leaders in its campaign: Gustav Stresemann, of the National Liberals, was already a sort of parliamentary spokesman for the army (**196**); and in the autumn of 1916 the Centre leader, Erzberger, was converted to the necessity of lifting restrictions on the sinking of neutral merchantmen (**48**). In January 1917 the Emperor, Bethmann Hollweg's last prop, came round to the OHL's way of thinking. Hindenburg clinched the matter by threatening to resign; and in February restrictions were lifted. The inevitable result was United States entry into the War on 6 April. America's industrial and financial might, added to its vast reserves of manpower, were more than enough to tip the balance against Germany and its increasingly exhausted allies (**201**; **209**; **55**).

In the meantime Bethmann Hollweg had dug his own political grave, by floating the idea of a serious reform of the Prussian suffrage, to the horror of Hindenburg and Ludendorff (**220**). The OHL responded by demanding the most extreme formulation of German war aims yet, the Kreuznach programme of April 1917, partly in the hope that the announcement of such goals would allay political unrest. But increasing war-weariness instead led to an upheaval on the political scene, when a minority within the SPD broke away to form the Independent Social Democratic Party (*USPD**)and declared themselves for an immediate end to the War, and a peace without annexations (**219**). To prevent the majority Social Democrats from making a similar declaration to retain working-class support, Erzberger drafted the Peace Resolution of July 1917, which called on the government to negotiate a peace without 'forced annexations'. Ambiguous though this was, it was seized upon by the OHL as proof that Bethmann Hollweg had 'lost control' of the Reichstag, and the Chancellor was forced to resign on 13 July (**55**; **218**; **48**) [**doc. 36**].

The period after the fall of Bethmann Hollweg saw the undisputed supremacy of the general staff and of military considerations in the formulation of policy. Bethmann Hollweg's successor, Georg Michaelis, was a biddable bureaucrat; and although the Bavarian Centre politician, Count Georg von Hertling, who took over in October 1917, was more his own man, there was little he could do against the iron will of the generals. Increased powers were given to the army: namely, restrictions on the right of assembly, surveillance of meetings, conscription of political agitators, and the use of army units to break strikes. All this merely served to heighten alienation, and the strikes continued: in the great strike of January 1918 some one and a half million workers participated (**209**; **219**).

More effective was the encouragement the OHL gave to the formation of the German Fatherland Party (*DVP**) in September 1917. The DVP was the first attempt to recruit mass party political support for the sort of ideas which characterised the radical nationalist right before 1914, and which the War had intensified. Chaired by Tirpitz and Wolfgang Kapp, a Prussian civil servant, the DVP called for huge annexations. It was launched with the aid of army propaganda service funds, supplemented generously by the Association of Iron and Steel Industrialists; and within a year its membership stood at some one and a half million. The DVP's appeal was certainly not just to the conservative elite and radical nationalists, but also to the farming community and above all to the impoverished middle class. It is significant that Anton Drexler, who founded the original German Workers' Party eventually taken over by Hitler, should have made his political debut as a DVP organiser (**173**).

The prospects for German victory seemed dim by the autumn of 1917. There was no solution to the food shortage, and Germany was surrounded by more enemies than ever before. Already in the OHL there was talk of being 'stabbed in the back' by the civilian politicians, and of the necessity of finding a suitable scapegoat for the army's failure (**208**). Then, in early November, came a sudden reprieve, in the shape of the Bolshevik Revolution in Russia. This not only enabled Germany to reach an armistice along the whole eastern front, thus giving a tremendous boost to morale; it also seemed to provide the army leadership with the last convincing evidence that they could win the War after all, in advance of the arrival of large numbers of American troops in Europe (**162**). Ludendorff prepared for an all-out offensive on the western front which began on 21 March 1918.

War aims

It is undeniable that Germany's enemies also had war aims. Russia wanted control of the Straits; France, the left bank of the Rhine; Italy, large chunks of the Habsburg Monarchy; and Britain and Japan, Germany's African and Pacific colonies. With the exception of Russia, moreover, the Allies attained these aims in one way or another. Yet German war aims differed fundamentally from those of the Allies in their territorial and economic range; in their disregard for ethnic boundaries in the pursuit of hegemony; and in their ideological nature, particularly in the East, where the *Lebensraum* mentality came to fruition (**202**; **201**; **173**). German aims, too, were ambitious right from the start, and as the War progressed became more and more extreme. To some extent this was because, as Bethmann Hollweg put it, appetite comes with eating (**38**), but the fact remains that German appetites were voracious, and demonstrably more so than those of the Allies.

From the outbreak of war, not only the military, but princes of the federal states, political and industrial leaders, and a formidable assortment of academics and pressure groups, began suggesting what Germany should demand. At the core of most of these plans was the concept of *Mitteleuropa**, a continent dominated politically and economically by Germany (**201**; **215**). And central to virtually everyone's idea of *Mitteleuropa* were annexations, whether for the defensive purpose of safeguarding Germany from future 'aggression', or as a springboard for further expansion. The King of Bavaria revived medieval claims to the whole of Belgium, and squabbled with the King of Saxony over who had the better title to be King of a restored Poland (**206**). None of the major parties, with the exception of the SPD, seemed to find anything fantastic in the annexation of non-German-speaking territory in both East and West; and even some Social Democrats succumbed to the idea of limited annexations as 'compensation' (**202**; **219**). The Pan-Germans, acting in concert with leading industrialists' groups like the CVDI and BdI, clamoured for western territory to secure industrial resources, and for eastern territory to ensure agricultural self-sufficiency (**202**; **87**). A 'Petition of the Intellectuals' in July 1915 made similar demands; the 1,300 signatures in support of this far out-numbered a counter-petition organised by the historian Hans Delbrück, protesting against the unnaturalness of such annexations (**223**; **192**).

The first official expression of war aims, and a clear reaction to some of these demands (**162**; **225**), was the so-called September Programme of 1914. Drafted at a time when victory in France was still confidently expected, it concentrated on what the government hoped to achieve in the West. There was no attempt to outline eastern aims in detail, although the Programme made clear that 'Russia must be thrust back as far as possible from Germany's eastern frontier and her domination over the non-Russian vassal peoples broken'. The immediate intention, however, was to leave France 'so weakened as to make her revival as a great power impossible for all time' (**201**, p. 103).

Fischer and his followers have unduly stressed the significance of the September Programme, arguing that government aims were ultimately no different from those of extremists like the Pan-German League, a claim disproved by comparison with Pan-German aims. But critics of Fischer have erred equally in dismissing the Programme as merely an *ad hoc* response to the situation (**142**, vol. 3). The essential fact is that the September Programme was conceivable at all. For France, it envisaged the annexation of certain strategically important towns, and of the Briey iron fields, a war indemnity, and 'the creation of a continuous Central African colonial empire' (**201**, p. 104). In Belgium, Germany was to control the coast, and would annex Liège and a frontier strip. Even more significant was the explicit intention of making not only France, Belgium and Luxembourg but also Holland 'economically dependent on Germany'. Although France was not defeated in the autumn of 1914, the German government continued to draw up detailed plans for a peace settlement [**doc. 37**]. If Bethmann Hollweg's goal was a form of European economic imperialism [**doc. 38**], his formulation of these 'moderate' aims could only act as an incentive to far more rabid annexationists.

Germany's western war aims remained stillborn because of the failure to achieve victory, and attention increasingly turned towards the East. As a result of German advances by late 1915, the central powers controlled all of Russian Poland and the Baltic coast almost to Riga. This gave a hitherto unthought-of plausibility to the advocates of *Lebensraum*, who could point to territory for agriculture and settlement already at Germany's disposal, and the possibility of acquiring more. Ludendorff was by 1915 a fervent partisan of huge annexations: apart from its strategic value, such territory, suitably colonised, would serve for inevitable future wars with the Slavs (**230**) [**doc. 39**]. Nor was Ludendorff on his own. As early as September 1914 the Pan-Germans were calling for the annexation of the Baltic provinces and most of Russian Poland. Territories formally annexed were to be cleared of their inhabitants and resettled with Germans; a special ghetto state would be created from more Russian territory for the Jews (**87**). As long as Bethmann Hollweg was Chancellor, however, the stress in Germany's war aims remained more on economic imperialism, on *Weltpolitik* through selective annexations, than on massive expansion in the interests of *Lebensraum* (**173**).

At first the government acknowledged none of its annexationist aims publicly, for fear this would alienate neutral opinion abroad, as well as moderate and left-wing opinion at home. But Bethmann Hollweg's defeat by Hindenburg and Ludendorff in December 1916, over the Peace Note to President Wilson, highlighted the ambiguity of his position. He simply could not announce that Germany would make no annexations. Those who regarded the war as purely defensive found this disturbing, and throughout the first half of 1917 pressure grew in the Reichstag, especially in the SPD and USPD, for clarification. The final impetus towards the Peace Resolution of July came after the OHL compelled Bethmann Hollweg to accept the Kreuznach Programme in April. This was the most radical yet, even if the Chancellor only signed it in the belief that such aims were unobtainable. The OHL demanded annexation of the Baltic provinces, all of Poland, France's Longwy-Briey coal and iron fields, Luxembourg and south Belgium; economic control of Belgium and the Roumanian oil-fields; and territorial compensation for its allies Austria-Hungary and Bulgaria in the Balkans. Kreuznach helped destroy what little support Bethmann Hollweg had in the Reichstag; and with his fall in July 1917 the way was clear for the 'triumph of *Lebensraum*' (**173**, p. 187).

There was now no possibility of a negotiated peace, let alone one without annexations. That autumn, the DVP was founded specifically to mobilise public support for control of the Dutch and Belgian coast, a Central African colonial empire and economic expansion into Russia and the Middle East (**173**). Then, the Bolshevik Revolution presented the *Lebensraum* imperialists with a golden opportunity to put their ideas into practice.

The Treaty of Brest-Litovsk of 18 March 1918 betrayed the full scope of German war aims. Russia formally ceded Poland, Lithuania and Courland (southern Latvia). Livonia (northern Latvia) and Estonia remained under German 'protection', with little likelihood of the Reich ever relinquishing provinces which contained even a sprinkling of ethnic Germans. A separate peace which the Germans

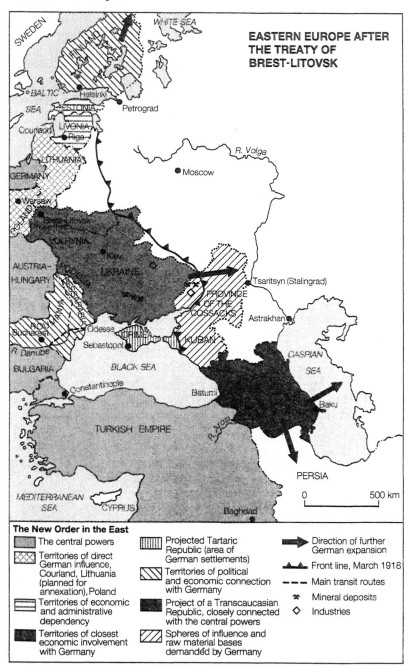

EASTERN EUROPE AFTER THE TREATY OF BREST-LITOVSK

The New Order in the East

- The central powers
- Territories of direct German influence, Courland, Lithuania (planned for annexation), Poland
- Territories of economic and administrative dependency
- Territories of closest economic involvement with Germany
- Projected Tartaric Republic (area of German settlements)
- Territories of political and economic connection with Germany
- Project of a Transcaucasian Republic, closely connected with the central powers
- Spheres of influence and raw material bases demanded by Germany
- Direction of further German expansion
- Front line, March 1918
- Main transit routes
- ✱ Mineral deposits
- ◇ Industries

concluded in February, with a separatist government in the Ukraine, was accepted by the Russians. German control of this huge puppet state was an essential part of the OHL's strategy, since the Ukraine was a fertile grain producer. In addition the German government signed treaties with secessionist governments in Finland and Georgia; the latter gave Germany access to the oil supplies of the Caucasus. Nor was the *Lebensraum* element neglected: as late as July, Ludendorff was planning German settlement in the Ukraine and Transcaucasia (**201**; **229**; **7**).

Brest-Litovsk was the ultimate expression of expansionist, radical nationalism in Wilhelmine Germany, and its effects were baleful. It deluded the German people into thinking victory was just around the corner, with the result that the shock of the eventual collapse in November 1918 was all the greater. It raised bitter resentment not only in Russia but also among the other peoples of eastern Europe, who could see that German rule was unlikely to be better than Russian. Resistance to German control in the Ukraine and Poland still had one and a half million troops tied down in the East when Ludendorff launched his great March offensive in the West (**20**). Most important, it inspired Germany's remaining enemies to even greater resistance, since if Germany could impose such terms in the East, why not also in the West? This is the real vindication of Fischer's thesis: when the German leadership got the chance, it *did* implement its war aims.

Defeat and revolution

At the time of Ludendorff's spring offensive the balance of forces on the western front was roughly equal, and for some weeks it seemed as if the German attack would carry all before it. Yet although the Allied armies were thrown back and disordered they were not broken; and by June the German advances had petered out. Without further reserves to commit, the German army was vulnerable to an Allied counter-attack. Britain and France could draw on greater reserves than Germany, but the decisive factor was the arrival of more Americans. Only 300,000 in France in March 1918, by July they numbered 1,200,000. When Allied forces attacked in early August the German army was in no condition to resist effectively, and a steady retreat began.

The German public was carefully kept in the dark as to the true nature of the situation, but despite this war-weariness had already become widespread. Yet until quite late in the War, the general distress expressed itself mainly through food riots and strikes over wages, rather than demands for political reforms or changes in government policy. There was seemingly little popular interest in revolutionary change. The Spartakus League, founded early in the War by Rosa Luxemburg and Karl Liebknecht, was unambiguously anti-war and revolutionary, but it remained a banned organisation (**226**) [**docs. 40a, b**].

The real potential for change, in so far as the OHL's determination to wage the War against hopeless odds was concerned, was in the morale of the armed forces, particularly the army. With the failure of Ludendorff's offensive, and the beginning of unremitting Allied attacks, the general war-weariness finally began to transform itself into demoralisation, and an unwillingness to die in prolonging a pointless struggle [**doc. 40c**].

At the same time something like a realistic appraisal of the situation was beginning to filter through at the OHL and in the government. One of the first to air his belief that the army had reached the limits of its endurance, ironically, was the Emperor William II, who throughout the War had led a shadowy, cocooned existence, firmly relegated to the background by an OHL only too aware of his real deficiencies as a warlord (**4**). Although the Emperor called a council at Spa on 14 August in an attempt to end the fighting, his personality was hardly strong enough to overcome the innate optimism of Hindenburg and Ludendorff (**209**). But by the end of September even Ludendorff was temporarily compelled to face reality. The decisive point was the capitulation of Bulgaria. This meant that Germany's access to Roumanian oil would be choked off, with grave consequences for its ability to wage what was increasingly a mechanised war. Ludendorff's nerve suddenly buckled, and on 29 September, in agreement with Hindenburg, he informed the Emperor and the Chancellor that an immediate armistice was essential. Even more startling, the generals also insisted on the introduction of a parliamentary form of government, which alone, they now said, would make it possible to negotiate peace terms [**doc. 41**].

It was typical of the OHL's relationship with the government that, having left the civilians in ignorance of the situation up to the last moment, it now demanded a ceasefire. It was also characteristic that Hindenburg and Ludendorff, while reluctantly accepting that Germany would probably have to renounce its aims in the West in order to conclude peace, were adamant that there could be no renunciation of German gains in the East. Chancellor Hertling was so shaken by this revelation of failure that he resigned on the spot; he was also genuinely unwilling to be associated with democratisation. Prince Max of Baden, the eldest son of one of the federal princes, consented to act as Chancellor on 3 October (**35; 214**).

The role played by the political parties in this has been the subject of controversy. Prince Max was able to take office because the two main parties in the Reichstag, the SPD and Centre, together with the Progressives, were willing to assure him a parliamentary majority (**212**). The motives of the OHL and in particular Ludendorff, however, were sinister. To Ludendorff it was precisely these parties which had encouraged internal dissent, and in his view it was this internal weakness *alone* which had prevented a total victory (**208; 209**). Ludendorff's demand that the parties be brought into government was part of a conscious design to shift the blame for defeat onto the politicians [**doc. 42**]. In seeking an armistice it is also clear that the OHL did not exclude the possibility of using it merely as a breathing-space, and resuming hostilities at some later date. Parliamentarisation, followed by armistice, was thus a screen behind which the OHL could make its preparations, as a Bavarian officer reported to Munich, 'to swing into the saddle again and rule on according to the old prescription' (**199**, p. 516).

Germany's brief experience of parliamentary monarchy, however, frustrated Ludendorff's plans for a military comeback. On 4 October, Prince Max addressed a note to President Wilson, offering a ceasefire. At home he rapidly agreed with the Reichstag on two essential amendments to the constitution, by which the Chancellor and his government were required to have the confidence of the Reichstag, and the Emperor was divested of his absolute control over army and navy appointments. A number of other amendments consolidated the new supremacy of the Reichstag, which also opened the way for reform of the Prussian constitution (**222**).

Meanwhile the new regime had claimed its first victory. President Wilson's reply to the peace note, on 16 October, stipulated that a ceasefire would have to be preceded by an immediate cessation of unrestricted submarine warfare. He added on the 23rd that the precondition of any armistice must be the assurance that Germany could not resume hostilities. It was Ludendorff's bitter defence of submarine warfare which forced his resignation on 26 October, since Prince Max, assured of the support of the Reichstag, could threaten the Emperor with his own resignation if the OHL did not give way.

Hindenburg, despite his reluctance to abandon submarine warfare, could see the way the wind was blowing and remained at his post (**209**; **214**).

Throughout October, however, circumstances worked against the survival of Prince Max's government. As soon as it became public knowledge that it was seeking a ceasefire, there was a vast change in popular attitudes. OHL propaganda had left people unprepared for the sudden change in fortunes. Once an end to the War seemed near, the impatience of ordinary Germans, and especially those in the armed forces, for an end to privations and danger became a political factor of real importance. The new government seemed too little of a break with the past, and appeared to be doing nothing to hasten peace. Above all, William II, the figure most intimately, if erroneously, linked with the failures of the War, was still there. Although by late October there was a growing consensus in political and even army circles that the Emperor would have to step down, this was not known publicly (**35**; **222**).

The final impetus towards revolution was provided by the navy. Ever since its reorganisation in August 1918 under a unified Naval War Command (*SKL**), comparable to the army's OHL, the navy under Admiral Reinhard Scheer had been showing a new political energy (**195**). Historians are still debating the reasons behind the SKL's order of 29 October to the high seas fleet to prepare for a sortie into the North Sea. Whether this was a collective death-wish by officers more concerned with their professional honour than the lives of their crews (**204**), or an attempt to bring down the government and introduce a military dictatorship by sabotaging the armistice negotiations (**209**; **203**), the effect on the fleet's sailors was unambiguous. The crews mutinied, and by 4 November had taken over Kiel and proclaimed a 'sailors' council'.

The sailors were primarily concerned with self-preservation, but since the Kiel council also proclaimed its wish for a peace without annexations or indemnities, it started a trend. Councils of soldiers, sailors and workers sprang up all over Germany, with the USPD and the SPD trying desperately to establish some form of political control over them in the hope of preserving order and forestalling a Bolshevik-style takeover. What was happening was a radicalisation of the political climate, with the obvious popular impatience at the failure to sign an armistice dragging the SPD, especially, towards a decisive break with the government (**221**).

It was the seizure of power in Munich on 7–8 November by the Bavarian USPD leader, Kurt Eisner, which pushed the SPD over the brink. The SPD leadership was still hoping to save the monarchy, but they now informed Prince Max that they could not remain in his government if the Emperor did not abdicate. Although Prince Max was willing to comply, William had fled to army headquarters, indulging in wild fantasies of marching back to Berlin at the head of what he persisted in regarding as his loyal troops. It was left to General Wilhelm Groener to convince the Emperor that the army did not stand behind him, and William fled into exile in Holland on 9 November. But it was by now too late even to save the monarchy. Revolution had broken out in Berlin the same day, with the election of a soldiers' council. The SPD withdrew from the government of Prince Max, who resigned in favour of Friedrich Ebert, the party leader. Ebert's colleague, Philipp Scheidemann, for fear of being upstaged by the USPD, proclaimed a republic that afternoon. It was with the republic that the Allies finally signed the armistice on 11 November (**222**; **212**).

Part Three: Assessment

Germany had clearly lost the War, and it had done so at a cost of some six million dead and wounded. By the Treaty of Versailles, it was forced to cede substantial territory, which involved a further loss of some six and a half million people, of whom roughly half were German-speaking. The Treaty also required Germany to accept responsibility for the War, and hence financial liability for damage incurred by the Allies.

Despite this, within two decades Germany had re-emerged as the dominant power on the European continent and, twenty years after Versailles, unleashed another war on its neighbours. The National Socialist regime was one of the most frightening dictatorships in human history, and it came to power in 1933 on a wave of discontent, some of which was directly attributable to the effects of the First World War; while its radical nationalism went back even further in German history. Thus it is important to determine just what continuities, as well as discontinuities, exist.

Germany after 1890 contrasts with the Bismarckian period in a number of significant ways. Although the foundations of economic growth were laid long before unification, it is the period after 1890 which is the one of most startling change. A combination of circumstances made Germany, by 1914, the premier industrial power on the Continent; and it is clear that, had it not been for the War, the country would have attained peacefully the economic hegemony, or German-dominated *Mitteleuropa*, that the proponents of *Weltpolitik* dreamed of. In military terms, too, Wilhelmine Germany was a far more formidable power than Bismarck's Reich: its population continued to grow; its army was the most powerful and effective, if not the largest on the Continent; and by 1914 it possessed the second largest navy in the world.

These were positive changes, at least from the viewpoint of the average German. In terms of overall political direction, however, Wilhelmine Germany can be said to have suffered something like a relapse compared with the preceding period. Bismarck had at least provided some central direction to the affairs of the Empire, but the constitution he had drafted for Germany was flawed from the start. The apparatus of control given to the federal government, especially in the financial realm, was too sketchy for such a large and complex society. By 1890 Bismarck was contemplating drastic remedies for the dilemma he had created; Germany was simply bursting the bounds of the Bismarckian constitution. The personality of William II could only increase this chaos at the top. The Emperor, as Röhl has recently reminded us (**10**), was undoubtedly crucial for certain highly significant developments, such as the navy, the furtherance of *Weltpolitik* and encouraging a spirit of industrial modernism; but he could lay down no consistent line, and the ministers he chose reflected this. Wilhelmine Germany was like a highly developed and versatile animal, hampered by a very small brain.

In the political sphere the gap between government and Reichstag persisted right down to 1914: the Reichstag could not really control the government, while the government could not legislate effectively without the Reichstag. This meant constant confrontation, rather than ungovernability, and by 1914 there were some signs of movement. By 1913 plans were being drawn up for collective ministerial responsibility in the federal government, comparable to the British cabinet system; there was widespread perception of the need for a reform of the Prussian suffrage; and even the SPD was beginning to look less alarming to government figures like Bethmann Hollweg. Recent research has shown that popular participation in the political process was increasing, even if the government was slow to respond to these pressures (**75**).

In contrast to Germany's political development, its social transformation in the Wilhelmine era was profound. Sustained growth produced predictable social problems, but these were to some extent mitigated by the tradition of state intervention and social legislation. The improvement in absolute terms of working-class conditions was reflected in the consistent moderation of the SPD and of German trades unions. German society was in fact more divided by the anti-socialist propaganda of its conservative elite, and by the potential for serious conflict with the national minorities.

The armed forces made a peculiar contribution to the fate of imperial Germany, since neither army nor navy was subject to effective political control. This was an especially serious matter in time of war, when the army at least was able to exert a disastrous political influence of its own. In peacetime the armed forces created a financial burden the federal government could ill afford, and which in turn led to political crisis; and the naval programme, in addition to being expensive, ruined Germany's international position. The special social status of the army remains a matter for debate. While it would be an exaggeration to describe Wilhelmine society as militaristic, military values undoubtedly played too prominent a role.

Germany's foreign policy was the expression of both its institutional chaos and the pressure to expand economically. Conflicting counsels in the formulation of policy, as well as the bullying tone of German diplomacy, were quintessentially Wilhelmine. Behind the confusion and bluster, however, lay a consistent interest in the economic pre-eminence of Germany in Europe, and in German influence in the outside world, in the extension of which the navy was an essential instrument. Less influential before the War, but increasingly attractive during it, was the preoccupation with *Lebensraum*, the territorial expansion of Germany's population and agricultural base. All these contributed to the alienation of Germany's neighbours, as well as arousing national expectations with little to show for them. Pre-war foreign policy culminated in the supreme blunder of July 1914, although this crisis differed from previous confrontations in that the government was fully conscious of the risk of war, and deliberately courted it.

In assessing Wilhelmine Germany it is important to bear in mind its comparability with other societies. There were positive as well as negative forces at work, and perhaps the most striking thing about the country's development, right down to 1914, given the institutional obstacles to positive change, was its open-endedness. Certainly Wehler's view of the Empire as the antechamber to National Socialism seems overly deterministic (**40**). Equally, the idea to be found in some recent works, that Germany was steadily turning into a parliamentary monarchy, is even more far-fetched (**32; 21**). What can be said is that it took the extraordinary conditions of war and defeat to produce the negative turning point in German history that led to Nazism.

The centrality of the War as a forcing-house for unhealthy tendencies is obvious. War naturally inflamed nationalist sentiment, including anti-Slav and anti-Semitic racism, and encouraged an interest in territorial expansion. The War also had significant economic effects: it fuelled inflation, increased the visibility of high-profit capitalism, and led to considerable industrial integration. The Social Democratic movement was split by the issue of peace and continued support for the government. Even more serious were the social divisions of the War. Whereas the breakdown of social barriers at the front created a natural camaraderie among ex-soldiers, this led to a divide between veterans and the rest of society. Most important was the impoverishment of small farmers and above all the middle class: by the end of the War there was an unusually large number of people embittered against both the rich and 'the workers'.

On top of all this there came the unexpected shock of defeat. This had the short-term consequence of bewilderment and a tendency to blame the ruling class, sentiments visited upon the Emperor William and the institution of monarchy. In the long term the affront to national feeling which defeat represented, given galling immediacy in the Versailles Peace Treaty, is impossible to underestimate. Yet the circumstances of Germany's surrender, deliberately contrived by the OHL, combined to reinforce the popular conviction that Germany's great power position was still intact, and recoverable. This perpetuated the so-called 'stab in the back' legend: Germany had not really been defeated, rather the German people had been denied victory by the 'left' and the weakness of the politicians.

The continuities between the Empire and the succeeding period were the survival of Germany's conservative elite; a foreign policy based on an expansionist, nationalist imperialism; a deep-rooted fear of the left, heightened by the example of the Bolshevik Revolution; and the prevalence of certain racial and social ideas, especially anti-Semitism.

The discontinuities were the emergence of a more representative political system, especially in former strongholds of privilege like Prussia; the position of the middle class, who under the Empire felt generally secure, and under Weimar decidedly insecure; and the removal of protection from agriculture, which became much more of a minority voice than it had been. In so far as there was potential for a more open political and social order before 1914, these positive elements in German society seemed to have won in 1918 and during the 1920s. But the apparent gains were from the start undermined by the continuities, now exaggerated by the effects of war and defeat. Hitler, as has often been pointed out, climbed to power with the aid of Germany's conservative elite; and the binding element between the old elite and the new nationalist forces created by the War, and which Hitler personified, was a belief in Germany's natural position as *the* European great power. This was perhaps the most fateful link of all between Wilhelmine Germany and the National Socialist dictatorship.

Part Four: Documents

Unless otherwise indicated, the translation of documents from the original German has been done by the authors of this volume.

document 1
The personality of William II

(a) *A speech at Königsberg in September 1894, to the representatives of East Prussia, shows William's obsession with subversion, and gives a good idea of his style.*

Before our eyes yesterday an elevating ceremony was played out; before us stands the statue of Emperor William I, the imperial sword raised in his right hand, a symbol of law and order. It reminds us all of other duties, of the serious struggle against the tendencies which are directed against the foundations of our existence as a state and a society. So, gentlemen, my appeal goes out to you now: *Forward in the struggle for religion, for morality and order, against the parties of revolution!*

   Just as ivy twines itself around the gnarled trunk of the oak, adorns it with its foliage and protects it, when storms roar through its crown, so does the Prussian nobility gather around My House. Let it, and with it the entire nobility of the German nation, become a shining example to those sectors of the populace which are still uncommitted. Well then! let us go forward together into this battle! Forward with God, and dishonour to him who forsakes his King!

Ernst Johann (ed.), *Reden des Kaisers: Ansprachen, Predigten und Trinksprüche Wilhelms II* (Munich, 1966), pp. 62–3.

(b) *This exchange with Chancellor Hohenlohe in March 1897 illustrates the Emperor's personal commitment to the navy and his contempt for the Reichstag and non-Prussians.*

To my surprise H[is] M[ajesty] received me with great affability, listened assentingly to my explanation, and then indulged himself in a highly detailed lecture on the navy. . . . He enumerated the ships we have and the ones we would need in order to survive a war;

... emphasised that we had to have an armoured fleet to protect our trade and keep ourselves supplied with provisions; and was of the opinion that our fleet would have to be strong enough to prevent the French fleet cutting off the food supplies we needed. In addition, he ... would have to find the means, and if the Reichstag didn't approve this, he would nevertheless carry on building and present the Reichstag with the bill later. Public opinion didn't concern him. He knew that people didn't love him, and cursed him; but that wouldn't deter him. I then reminded the Emperor of the difference between Prussia and the Empire; said that in Prussia he had old rights which continued to exist, so far as the Prussian constitution had not limited [them]. In the Empire the Emperor only had the rights which the Reichstag conceded to him. The Emperor interjected 'the Emperor hardly has any rights', which I attempted to refute. Besides, this was quite unimportant, said HM: the South German democratic states didn't worry him. He had 18 army corps and would make short work of the South Germans.

Furst Chlodwig zu Hohenlohe-Schillingsfürst, *Denkwürdigkeiten der Reichskanzlerzeit*, ed. K. A. von Müller (Stuttgart, 1931), p. 311.

(c) *Baroness Spitzemberg was a well-connected political hostess. An entry from her diary for 1903 throws light on William's ambitions and on conservative opposition.*

14 March. Thursday I had breakfast at the Harrachs', only with Kurt Kessel. . . . He had various things to relate: incidents in the higher administration and party politics, which sound very disturbing, but which unfortunately must be true, since he had most of it direct from Theobald Bethmann [Hollweg], who is not only a highly important man, but is very closely connected with the Emperor, but is not one of his blind admirers. According to him, those who call the Emperor's policy indecisive do him an injustice. His first, most fundamental idea is to break Britain's world position in favour of Germany; for this he needs a fleet; in order to have that, a lot of money; and since only a rich country can provide this, Germany must become rich; hence the preference he shows industry and his rage at the landowners who, in order not to go under, are defending themselves against this policy. Also consistent . . . is a remark of HM recently . . . which disturbingly has become public knowledge; he said there, he hardly regarded the Social Democrats as a danger, he'd easily deal with them, for him there were much

more dangerous enemies, who were thrusting a spoke into his wheel, the Farmers' League. . . . It is hardly worth putting arguments against the above convictions of the Emperor, there are so many which have a claim to be considered; . . . [he] completely forgets that, as a continental power, we can never let our army be weakened, whereas army and navy together are devouring us. In addition a growing industry pulls more and more people into the towns and in the process abandons them to the Social Democrats. Such a thoroughly mistaken . . . idea is really more disastrous than an indecisive course, if it is held by a person as powerful as our Emperor; a little megalomania, *i.e.* the ambition to create something quite different from what his grandfather created, is . . . in my view, the mainspring of the Emperor's behaviour. The grandfather founded the German Empire with the army; he wants to make Germany a commercial and colonial power with the fleet. As long as our future, instead of taking to the waves, doesn't sink beneath them and come to nought in the process. . . .

Das Tagebuch der Baronin Spitzemberg . . . ed. Rudolf Vierhaus (Göttingen, 1960), pp. 427–8.

document 2

Exporting goods – or people

In 1891, defending his trade treaties in the Reichstag, Caprivi made clear his belief that the expansion of trade and industry was vital to support Germany's growing population.

Trade and industry are . . . the most essential sources of prosperity and with it of political power and cultural importance; for without a certain degree of prosperity the arts and sciences . . . will not be able to flourish. . . .

The working class is bound together with industry most intimately, and we would have neglected our duty, if we had not, in concluding these treaties, kept the possibility of preserving our working class, preserving their ability to be productive, steadily before us. Two factors then came up for discussion; first, to procure cheaper foodstuffs. In so far as that could take place without endangering state interests . . . the federated governments . . . have effected the lowering of the tariff on foodstuffs which they considered permissible. For the preservation and prosperity of the working class, however, I regard it as far more essential that work should be found for them. (*Quite right! from the Right.*) If this were not the more essential question, then the rush of our rural labourers to the cities and to the West could hardly be explained. Our West always has prices for indispensable foodstuffs which are so much higher than in the East (*Quite right! from the Left.*) that, if we compare these prices . . . , we have to conclude that there must be a continuous rise in the cost of living in the West. That people, in spite of this, move so readily westwards, is because they can set higher wages against a cheaper cost of living. Remunerative jobs, however, will, if these treaties are accepted, . . . be found. We will find them by means of export; we must export: either we export goods, or we export people. With this mounting population, and without a comparably growing industry, we are not in a position to survive any longer.

Fenske (**2**), pp. 35–6.

document 3

The agrarian interest strikes back

A Silesian tenant-farmer, Ruprecht-Ransern, was one of the driving forces behind the creation of the Farmers' League. In an article in December 1892 he called on agrarians to resist the Caprivi treaties.

We must cry out, so that the whole nation hears us, we must cry out until we are heard in the chambers of parliament and the ministries – we must cry out until it reaches the steps of the throne! But we must at the same time act, so that our cry does not once again die away unnoticed. We must act by ceasing to do what up to now we always considered a matter of course: running the elections for the government in our districts; we must lay down all honorary appointments, to which we cannot legally be bound; we must bring things to the point where our district council presidents report to their superiors: 'The greatest discontent dominates the farmers' circles, and their previous attitude, that was so well disposed to the government, has turned into the reverse. . . .'

I propose nothing more or less than that we go among the Social Democrats and present a serious front against the government; show it that we are not inclined to let ourselves be treated so badly any further, as before; and let them feel our power.

Schulthess' europäischer Geschichtskalendar, 34 (1893), pp. 5–6.

Moderation of the SPD

In 1891 the Bavarian Social Democrat Georg Vollmar outlined his party's stance now that Bismarck's anti-socialist legislation had lapsed.

... our tactics today cannot be the same as during the state of emergency. In any case we never gave up parliamentary activity and participation in daily politics even at the time; only the Party's principal task then had to consist of the bitterest, grimmest resistance against a government, which placed us outside the law, was trying to destroy us politically and individually, and hence with whom there could only be war, not negotiation. Nowadays it is different. The government has probably not given up the struggle against us. But the barbaric war of annihilation is over, and they have recognised us as a belligerent power and are conducting a civilised fight against us, in which, by our ability, we are in a position to achieve real successes.

Fenske (**2**), p. 29.

'Reconcile, pacify, rally, unite'

In 1897 Bülow described to Eulenburg his relationship with the Emperor, as well as his conception of foreign policy.

Everything which is done for our dear, dear master is according to your way of thinking, and He is constantly in my mind, is motive and goal for me, the *raison d'être* in everything.

The higher and more ugly the waves of misunderstanding, hate, envy beat against Him – and in this regard the situation even now is very difficult and very serious – the more I feel myself drawn to Him. I will never ever seek my own honour, but only His welfare. . . .

I lay the main stress on foreign policy. . . . Only a successful external policy can help, reconcile, pacify, rally, unite. Its preconditions are of course caution, patience, tact, reflection. . . . It is not a good idea to sound a victory fanfare before the definitive victory, excessive sabre-rattling annoys without frightening. The main thing remains steadiness and a sense of proportion *i.e.* neither offending foreign powers – Russia as well as Britain – unnecessarily, nor making [them] insolent by all too lively advances.

I am completely open, sincere and honest with our dear master. But I don't mean to play the schoolmaster towards him. First because it hurts me to see His beautiful eyes sad, but then also because for Him everything depends on His ... retaining trust and friendship for me. I am entering more and more into His ideas, am trying to turn everything round for the best.

John C. G. Röhl (ed.), *Philipp Eulenburgs politische Korrespondenz*, vol. 3 (Munich, 1983), pp. 1877–8.

document 6

A contemporary view of *Sammlungspolitik*

In an essay published in 1899, an adviser to Admiral Tirpitz saw Sammlungspolitik *as a trade-off between agrarians and industrialists.*

The combatants at one extreme, the opponents of social reform, sit in a particular quarter of the agrarian and heavy industrialists' camp, next to a section of high finance, as well as in certain circles of the so-called liberal middle class and a few groups of the bureaucracy and the judiciary.

... The large landowner wants high grain tariffs and wants to prevent measures of social reform being applied to the countryside, which could make his workers more expensive or demanding. He also does not want to strengthen the peasant proprietor class at the expense of landed property. The heavy industrialist wants a powerful protection for his business, sufficient to secure him the domestic market and enable him to compete in the world market with the surplus of his manufactures. He wants, furthermore, to be master in his own factory, with regard to working conditions and wage levels. If he can regulate the latter, and thereby control the size of his net profit, then agricultural protective tariffs and the consequent increase in production costs are not all that uncomfortable for him. This is what we call the policy of 'rallying'.

Ernst von Halle, *Volks- und Seewirtschaft: Reden und Aufsätze* (Berlin, 1902), vol. 2, pp. 214–15.

document 7

The failure of anti-socialist legislation

Posadowsky confessed the pointlessness of attempting further repressive legislation in a speech to the Reichstag in December 1899.

The comments which have been made against the federated governments during the general debate remind me strongly of an article which I found some time ago. . . . There it was argued: We must have a strongman! That's what we're missing, and this strongman has the task of grabbing Social Democracy by the throat and throttling it. That was roughly the essential point. . . . If such a strongman exists in Germany, I wish that he would make an appearance in this Honourable House pretty soon (*prolonged laughter*), or, what would suit me even better, that he would be so kind as to turn up here in my place. This strongman . . . would very soon make the discovery that in a constitutional state one can only deal with a party, however much a government dislikes it, on the basis of existing laws (*Quite right!*), and that in a constitutional state one can only make laws with the help of the representatives of the people (*Quite right!*); and I very much doubt whether this strongman, in the present mood of the Honourable House, would succeed in negotiating laws, on the basis of which he would be able to grab Social Democracy by the throat and throttle it. (*Quite right!*)

Johannes Penzler and Ernst Ehrenberg (eds), *Graf Posadowsky . . . an der Hand seiner Reden*, vol. 2 (Leipzig, 1908), p. 235.

document 8

The financial dilemma

In a letter of January 1912 to Bethmann Hollweg, Treasury Secretary Wermuth spelt out the impossibility of funding both army and navy.

If there really is any way of effecting a reduction in the claims of army and navy, in all probability it will be because of the way the army's demands are sharply forced down by the navy's share. *I simply cannot abandon the conviction that Germany's position as a central European land power forces us to direct all our efforts towards the efficiency of the army.* The strengthening of the navy would be too dearly bought if it means forcing back the requirements of the army, especially if the resulting political complications are taken into account. . . . The financial administration, by all means, is bound to comply with the imperative needs of defence and to seek a compromise between defence interests and financial considerations. I believe I have more than fulfilled this duty. In . . . August 1910, I proposed vigorous action forthwith *in favour of the army;* but the suggestion, repeated several times, was not taken up at the time.

Adolf Wermuth, *Ein Beamtenleben: Erinnerungen* (Berlin, 1922), pp. 280–1.

document 9

German industry through British eyes

A publicist in 1896 drew the attention of the British public to what he considered Germany's alarming invasion of the home market.

You will find that the material of some of your own clothes was probably woven in Germany. Still more probable is it that some of your wife's garments are German importations; while it is practically beyond a doubt that the magnificent mantles and jackets wherein her maids array themselves on their Sundays out are German-made and German-sold, for only so could they be done at the figure. Your governess's *fiancé* is a clerk in the City, but he also was made in Germany. The toys, and the dolls, and the fairy books which your children maltreat in the nursery are made in Germany: nay, the material of your favourite (patriotic) newspaper had the same birthplace as like as not. Roam the house over, and the fateful mark will greet you at every turn, from the piano in your drawing-room to the mug on your kitchen dresser, blazoned though it be with the legend, *A Present from Margate.* Descend to your domestic depths, and you shall find your very drain-pipes German made. You pick out of the grate the paper wrappings from a book consignment, and they also are 'Made in Germany'. You stuff them into the fire, and reflect that the poker in your hand was forged in Germany. As you rise from your hearthrug you knock over an ornament on your mantlepiece; picking up the pieces you read, on the bit that formed the base, 'Manufactured in Germany'. And you jot your dismal reflections down with a pencil that was made in Germany. At midnight your wife comes home from an opera which was made in Germany, has been here enacted by singers and conductor and players made in Germany, with the aid of instruments and sheets of music made in Germany. You go to bed, and glare wrathfully at a text on the wall; it is illuminated with an English village church, and it was 'Printed in Germany'.

Ernest Edwin Williams, '*Made in Germany*' (London, 1896), pp. 10–11.

document 10

German industrial development by 1913

On the twenty-fifth anniversary of William II's accession, the banker Karl Helfferich celebrated the rise of German industrial power.

The industrial development of our time rests upon those two mighty pillars, coal and iron. Germany is one of the lands which nature has richly endowed with these two primary materials of industry. Germany also possesses considerable supplies of other important minerals especially salts, and zinc, lead, and copper ores. In recent generations we have learned how to recover these minerals and to utilise them more and more perfectly. During the past twenty-five years the value of the direct products of German mining . . . has increased from about 700,000,000 marks to considerably more than 2,000,000,000 marks. . . .

The year 1912 showed still further progress. The production of coal rose to 259,400,000 tons. . . .

Germany's coal production has accordingly been increased three-fold during the past twenty-five years.

Among producing countries Germany occupies the third place, after the United States and England. . . .

About one-fifth of the total coal production of the world today falls to Germany.

The expansion of the iron industry has been not less remarkable. . . .

The production of pig-iron in Germany during the past quarter of a century has . . . been increased more than four-fold.

Germany now occupies the second place among producing countries. . . .

The world's production of pig-iron now amounts to about 75,000,000 tons, of which about one-fourth falls to Germany.

Karl Helfferich, *Germany's Economic Progress and National Growth 1888–1913* (Berlin, 1913), pp. 60–3.

document 11

The second richest man in Prussia

The assets of this member of the aristocracy show that land was not the only source of great wealth in 1912.

Prince Guido Henckel von Donnersmarck is currently the second richest person in Prussia. . . .

. . . His entire landed property in Prussia comprises 23,295 hectares, with a total net yield from land tax of about 126,000 marks and a worth of 15 million marks. In addition, however, the Prince also possesses the estates of Tabkowice and Dobirzowice (altogether 1,125 hectares) in Russian Poland, and the manor of Lipowiec (altogether 3,076 hectares) in Galicia [Austria-Hungary].

The total landed property of the Prince therefore comprises a surface area of 27,496 hectares in Prussia, Russia and Austria. . . .

The other nine tenths of the Prince's property is principally based on the possession of coal mines; of industrial shares, particularly iron and zinc; of portions of construction firms, which the Prince regularly sets up in the form of limited companies; of banking shares, as well as from sleeping partnerships in warehouses and other businesses – finally, on the disposition over a cash capital of 12–15 million marks in interest-bearing deposits in major banks.

Ritter and Kocka (**6**), p. 372.

document 12

Upper middle-class ostentation

The following menu was served at a wedding reception in Hamburg in 1906. According to the groom, entertainment on this scale was nothing out of the ordinary in upper middle-class circles.

Caviar
Georg Goulet 1898 Extra Quality Dry
Consommé Mercédes
Paupiettes of Sole à la Prince Robert
Forster Jesuitengarten 1900
Smoked Fillet of Veal à la Duchesse d'Albany
Château Gironville 1888
Roe Cutlets à la réforme

Oberemmeler 1900
Heligoland Lobster en belle vue
Château Yquem 1900, estate bottled
Neige au Cliquot
Fresh Asparagus Tips with Truffles
Purée of Chicory à la crème
Holstein Pheasant
Château Margaux 1891, estate bottled
Bombe Mikado
Veuve Cliquot, England demi sec
Cheese Straws
Old Port Wine
Fruits
Dessert

Ritter and Kocka (**6**), p. 375.

document 13

The political attitude of big business

In a memorandum for William II on the Ruhr miners' strike in 1912, the steel industrialist Krupp demonstrated his reactionary beliefs as well as his links with the imperial family. (Emphasis by Krupp underlined; by William in italics.)

It appears at least doubtful whether, in view of political circumstances nowadays, the Social Democrats' power can still be seriously and lastingly shaken at all by political means.

In these circumstances there is really only one area where the Social Democrats *might suffer* severe and perhaps *decisive defeats*: that is the area of *industrial disputes* undertaken and promoted by them frivolously and for *purposes of agitation*. A few big strikes, ending in complete defeat for the workers, would *severely damage* the Social Democrats' prestige among the broad mass of the workers, in circumstances so serious, that the *suggestion* of their irresistible triumph, with which they now draw the masses in their wake, *could* perhaps by this means *be broken*. . . .

The employers demand and expect only one thing: namely, that in *this struggle the State does not once again restrain* them; *that ministers do not come* to the strike area *in order to mediate*, which in every case *works in favour of the employees*; [William's marginal note: 'Agreed. This must stop!'] that in the Reichstag and Landtag *no statements be made from the dispatch box* which work *to the disadvantage of the employers* and *give hope of state intervention* to the workers; in short, that the authorities *merely remain onlookers* in the struggle and confine their activities under all circumstances to *maintaining public order* wherever it is threatened, and protecting life, limb and property.

Ritter and Kocka (**6**), p. 413.

The working class

(**a**) *Among the many categories of agricultural workers were the farmhands or* Gesindestand. *An observer of 1898 described them in the eastern provinces.*

. . . one cannot apply the standards of conditions in central Germany to those regions, where people still work from 4:30 or 5 in the morning to sundown, in other words the eastern provinces. Here ploughboy and girl have the lightest duties of all those who live on landed estates. To be sure one usually reckons on: 3 o'clock – get up and feed the horses; 4:30 – move the animals out; half an hour for breakfast; an hour and a half for the midday meal, when half an hour for unharnessing and re-harnessing, feeding the horses, *etc.*, is not considered too much; half an hour for a light meal; and 9 o'clock in the evening, or even later, move back; then feed the animals till 10 o'clock; that makes 18–19 hours with 2 hours' rest. . . . On the estates in eastern Germany they work from sun-up to sundown even on the shortest days of the year, in other words from 6:30 in the morning to 3:30 in the afternoon, and in most cases the light meal break is left out. In view of all this it certainly seems desirable for conditions of employment to be easier in the East, even if only to deprive the Social Democrats of the telling opportunity for agitation which the 17 and 18 hour day offers them. . . .

Ritter and Kocka (**6**), p. 193.

(**b**) *In 1907 3.3 per cent of Germans worked in domestic service. A report of 1900 described the conditions for servant girls.*

The essential point about the housework done by the servant girls lies in the limitlessness of the hours worked. They are bound to their jobs day and night. The concept of overwork is unknown in servants' law, as is the concept of night work. A girl, who had to fetch several hundred extra coals from the cellar at 9 o'clock on a Sunday evening, even though there was already enough available for the next day, and who complained about it to the police, was told by the lieutenant handling the complaint: 'You have to carry out your duties, even if your masters ask you to do it in the middle of the night.' This remark is characteristic of today's servants' law. According to this the servant has to be at the service of his masters whether it is noon or midnight. . . .

Of the servant girls who have given evidence, approximately half, or 51.5%, work more than 16 hours; the other, lesser half work 12–16 hours and only approximately 2% less than 12 hours.

Ritter and Kocka (**6**), pp. 257–8.

The Poles **document 15**

(**a**) *A 1905 study laid bare the antagonism between Germans and Poles in the town of Posen (Poznań) in eastern Prussia.*

According to the census of 1905 the population . . . included 58,552 Germans and 78,309 Poles. Even if, in spite of the tension between the Polish majority and the German minority, the business of the town proceeds smoothly and the nationality conflict shows itself relatively seldom, this can be attributed above all to the three-class suffrage of the municipal statutes and to the poverty of the Poles. Since the present-day constitution of the town came into force, the Poles have always possessed only a quite small minority in the town council. . . . The Polish share of town councillors' seats only rarely exceeds a sixth; today it is less, although recently the Poles have considerably raised their tax contributions by the purchase of houses, and all the Polish councillors at the moment represent the third class. Nevertheless the Germans would be mistaken to regard this state of affairs as one which is going to last. The Poles, according to all appearances, are advancing irresistibly in their share of the town's population. The lower and middle class in Posen are becoming more and more Polonised; the Germans are holding their position in the upper classes, but the question is whether in the long run a strong citizenry can be recruited from among these classes alone.

Among the well-to-do German population the Jews today still hold first place; although they constitute only four per cent of the inhabitants, they contribute almost a fourth of the entire state income tax in Posen. However, they are dwindling more and more. . . .

As far as the nationalist antagonism is concerned, the three-class suffrage in Posen fulfils its task: it has proved itself to be a first-rate weapon for assuring the well-to-do Germans in Posen of their position in the municipal administration *vis-à-vis* the Polish masses.

Ritter and Kocka (**6**), pp. 428–9.

(**b**) *Bülow, who carried on the work of the Settlement Commission and passed the Expropriation Law, explained his Polish policy in 1914.*

The problem of our policy in the Eastern Marches is this: Shall we permit, shall we, by our inactivity, encourage the Eastern domains, i.e. Posen, West Prussia and certain parts of Upper Silesia and East Prussia, to slip once more from the grasp of German nationality, or not? Everyone who has national German feelings will answer that this must never happen, that it is the duty and the right of the Germans to maintain our national ownership in the East of Prussia, and, if possible, to increase it. . . .

The struggle for the land, which in its essentials is a struggle to permeate the eastern districts with a sufficient number of Germans, will always be the Alpha and Omega of our national German policy in the East. This must be supported by the struggle for German culture and education, and, above all, for the German language. We certainly do not wish to deprive the Pole of his mother tongue, but we must try to bring it to pass that, by means of the German language, he comes to understand the German spirit. In our policy of settlement we fight for German nationality in the East; in our policy with regard to the schools we are really fighting for Polish nationality which we wish to incorporate in German intellectual life. Here, again, we cannot proceed without severity. . . .

Prince Bernhard von Bülow, *Imperial Germany* (London, 1914), pp. 264–5, 270.

German rule in Alsace-Lorraine

Baron von Dallwitz, the new governor, made an official tour of the provinces in 1913. His reception showed both the disaffection of the inhabitants and the authorities' tendency to see subversion everywhere.

Everywhere the speeches I made were received in friendly fashion, the inhabitants showed themselves to be glad at my coming and expressed their wishes and concerns frankly. Looked at superficially the impression of a particularly friendly cooperation and a loyal disposition intentionally displayed could have banished all other impressions.

Nevertheless there was no shortage of symptoms capable of arousing certain misgivings. The applause accorded me was too uniform, the decoration of the streets with flags, triumphal arches and the like too similar, to be taken for the spontaneous demonstrations of the people's mood.

... I was therefore especially struck by the expression of a country teacher, who had conducted his charges to the reception in frock-coat and white tie and received a few friendly words addressed to him in the most respectful way, to be sure, but with such a sarcastic, overbearing expression on his face, that I drew the attention of Secretary of State Count Roedern, who was accompanying me, to him.

A few weeks after the beginning of the War, then, on the occasion of a house-search, a letter from this teacher, whose name I had remembered at the time, was found, in which he wrote to the local clergyman more or less as follows: 'Today we saw the new Great Ox; we adorned him with flowers and greeted him with songs, now he undoubtedly believes that he has won the hearts of all Lorrainers.'

Gerhard von Mutius, 'Aus dem Nachlass des ehemaligen Kaiserlichen Statthalters ... von Dallwitz', *Preussische Jahrbücher*, 214 (1928), p. 302.

document 17
Mistreatment of a Danish Deputy

H. P. Hanssen, together with other prominent German Danes, was arrested on the outbreak of the War. Although, as a member of the Reichstag, he was soon released and the official responsible disciplined, the incident was symptomatic of how this minority had been treated in the past.

August 1, 1914. Yesterday Wolff's Bureau announced that Germany is in grave danger of war. . . . My son, who expects mobilization orders at any moment, was to come home to say good-bye. . . .

I had hardly reached home when I was called to the telephone. My bookkeeper informed me that Germany was said to be in a state of war, and that two of my associates on the *Hejmdal* [newspaper] . . . had been arrested, one on the street, the other in the newspaper office. The police had inquired about me at the same time. I quietly told my wife what was likely to happen and made some necessary arrangements with her.

At nine o'clock a car came speeding up. It stopped. Police-Sergeant Grün from Apenrade stepped out and walked up the hill towards my house. I went out to meet him. Courteously, ashamed, and half apologetically he told me that I was under arrest and ordered me to follow him. I bade farewell to my family, urged my son not to lose courage, and went with the officer.

Hans Peter Hanssen, *Diary of a Dying Empire*, ed. Ralph H. Lutz (Bloomington, Ind., 1955), pp. 7–8.

document 18
German nationalism and anti-Semitism

(a) *A pamphlet on anti-Semitism issued by the German Conservatives in 1894 made clear the extent to which such prejudice was socially acceptable.*

. . . although there is no longer a 'ghetto', in the larger cities we see Jews living almost exclusively together in entire streets, in commercial districts as well as upper-class residential areas; and instead of spreading out relatively evenly along the various rungs of the socio-economic ladder, they have applied themselves almost entirely to particular trades and thereby Judaicised these, instead of Germanising themselves. . . . One now sees, especially in the big cities, whole sections of commercial activity, for example the particularly profitable confectionery and clothing industries, given over to the Jews with such exclusivity that already there are hardly any non-Jews to be found there. But Jewry, supported by its wealth, pushes with similar lack of restraint into the leading intellectual classes, especially certain branches of university life, as well as literature and the press, and through this wins acceptance for the fact that it is quite systematically planning to displace our native population more and more from all lucrative and influential positions in our own civilisation. To advise 'patience', in the face of such a campaign, means to preach a cowardly, mute abandonment to national rape ... through centuries of long, hard labour we have built our house for ourselves, and not so that clever strangers can comfortably move in. And if Jewry, instead of assimilating with us, advances along the path of open conquest, then there can be no wrong, but only an act of justified self-defence, if we resolve to keep at least those positions which we still hold, especially officers' and administrators' jobs. We are not obliged to deliver up, without a murmur, not only our wealth but also our political leadership to a foreign race so strikingly different from us, and to set, so to speak, a Jewish head upon our Germanic body.

Fenske (**2**), pp. 86–7.

(**b**) *The Pan-German League represented more extreme German nationalists. In a 1912 pamphlet, Class suggested how to solve the 'Jewish question'.*

The recuperation of our national existence ... *is only possible if Jewish influence is either completely eliminated, or pushed back to an acceptable and safe level.* ...

Nowadays *it is absolutely imperative* that the *frontiers should be closed totally and ruthlessly against any further Jewish immigration;* ... *those foreign Jews, who have still not acquired citizenship, should be ruthlessly and as fast as possible deported, down to the last man* – but even that is not enough.

However hard it will be for the German sense of justice: *we must generally limit the rights of resident Jews.* ...

The demand must be: *Jews resident in the country will be placed under aliens' law.*

The preliminary question runs: *Who is a Jew?* ... *A Jew, in the sense of the required aliens' law, is every person who, on 18 January 1871, belonged to the Jewish religious community, as are all descendants of persons who were Jews at that time, even if only one parent was or is Jewish. . . .*

. . . but what should the aliens' law ordain? *. . .*

All *public appointments* will remain *barred* to the Jews. *. . .*

They will not be allowed to *serve in the army or in the navy.*

They will receive neither *active nor passive franchise.* The professions of *the law and teaching* will be prohibited to them; as will be the *management* of theatres.

Newspapers, where Jews work, will be labelled as such; the others, which we can call in general 'German' newspapers, will not be allowed either to be owned by Jews, nor to have Jewish managers.

Banks, which are not the purely personal businesses of individuals, will not be allowed to have Jewish managers.

Landed property will not be allowed in future either to be owned by Jews, or to be burdened by Jewish mortgages.

As recompense for the protection which Jews enjoy as aliens, they will pay twice the tax Germans do.

Daniel Frymann [Heinrich Class], *Wenn ich der Kaiser wär'* (Leipzig, 1912), p. 74.

document 19

The Schlieffen Plan

In a memorandum for Chief of the General Staff Moltke in 1912, Ludendorff summarised the Plan and its strategic implications.

In view of Germany's central position, and assuming the political situation in Europe does not change, we will always be obliged to wage war on several fronts, and hence will have to wage a defensive war on one front, with numerically weaker forces, in order to be able to go on the offensive on the other one. The latter enemy can never be any other than France. Here we can hope for a quick decision, whereas an offensive war carried into the heart of Russia would be without foreseeable end. In order to take the offensive against France, however, it will be necessary to violate Belgian neutrality. Only by an advance across Belgian territory can we hope to be able to attack and defeat the French army in the open. This way we will find the British Expeditionary Force and also – if we don't succeed in concluding a treaty with Belgium – the Belgian troops in front of us. All the same, this operation has greater prospects of success than a frontal attack on the fortified French eastern front. Such an attack would force us to resort to siege warfare tactics, would cost much time and would deprive the army of impetus and initiative, which we need all the more, the greater the number of enemies with whom we have to reckon.

W. Kloster, *Der deutsche Generalstab und der Präventivkriegs-Gedanke* (Stuttgart, 1932), p. 52.

document 20

The army expansion of 1912–13

As a result of the Balkan Wars, the general staff began to press for even more troops, but officials at the war ministry, like General Wandel, expressed reservations.

9.1.[1913]
Today a comprehensive discussion with representatives of the chief of the general staff revealed that the latter, in view of the military-political situation, is demanding a massive strengthening of the army over a period of only a few years, which should come to at least 100,000 men in peacetime. . . .

The war minister has a difficult decision ahead of him. In my personal opinion the demands of the general staff exceed requirements and are at this time militarily unrealisable. The need for officers would be so great that it would be impossible to meet it for the foreseeable future, the vacancies could therefore only be filled by a reduction in the number of officers with individual formations, which would be dangerous in both peace and war. . . .

Granier (**134**), pp. 142–3.

document 21

The army as an instrument of social control

In 1907 the general commanding the 8th Army Corps issued a directive to his commanders on 'Policy during Civil Disorders'.

In a real uprising it must be assumed that the insurgents are well organised; the Social Democratic cooperative societies and trade unions to be found everywhere are to some extent already a preparation for this.

The insurgents will also be abundantly provided with financial means, as well as with good, modern weapons. . . .

In street fighting, *infantry*, where possible, must be deployed with artillery. A frontal assault against barricades, without adequate preparation by means of artillery, exacts heavy casualties, and in fact often fails completely.

. . . an advance by infantry in open streets, under fire from barricades or from houses, must be avoided. Rather, troops must press forward step by step from one house to another by breaking through the walls, or advance through gardens and courtyards and over rooftops. . . .

The bayonet plays a large role in house fighting. . . .

Under no circumstances may senior or junior officers enter into negotiations with insurgents; the only terms possible are 'Unconditional Surrender'.

All ringleaders, or anyone taken with weapons in his hands, is liable to the death penalty. The full rigour of the law must be applied without mercy.

Dieter Fricke, 'Zur Rolle des Militarismus nach innen in Deutschland vor dem ersten Weltkrieg', *Zeitschrift für Geschichtswissenschaft*, 6 (1958), pp. 1303–5.

document 22

Military values in society

A Social Democrat made the following criticism in the Reichstag in 1914.

The historical development of Germany has resulted in the middle class becoming feudalised and militarised. (*Hear! Hear! from the Social Democrats.*) In many cases it is not the respectable citizen who is the current ideal for the middle class of the German people, but rather the dashing gentleman with *von* in front of his name with the turned-up moustaches. (*Laughter.*) In this country a young tradesman doesn't want to look like a young tradesman, but rather if possible like a lieutenant in civvies. (*Laughter.*) And a young man of the most middle-class origins, if he is ambitious, first gets himself a monocle, and then assumes that awe-inspiring royal Prussian upper-crust accent. (*Laughter.*) So it is no wonder that the middle class does not offer any energetic resistance to the duel, but rather, because of its sick, backward, retarded class consciousness, accommodates itself to this bad habit, precisely because it is feudal. . . .

Ritter and Kocka (**6**), p. 77.

The Zabern Incident

Bethmann Hollweg got a rough ride from the Reichstag over Zabern, but his speech of 3 December 1913 nevertheless upheld the army's special position.

. . . the military authorities will continue, and rightly, to uphold the view that they cannot tolerate insults which are inflicted upon them, (*Bravo! from the Right.*) and that they cannot do so especially in this case, where it has not just been a matter of a single isolated molestation but rather, according to what I have imparted to you, a whole chain of molestations following one after the other. (*Interjection from the Left: Continued provocation of the inhabitants!*) Whether there have been violations of the penal law; whether there are civil claims for compensation to be met, that the judge will have to decide. In any case, however, I beg you, gentlemen, not to forget that, even in this serious and in many respects very sad case, the army has the right to protect itself against direct attacks. (*Interjection from the Social Democrats: The attacks were made by children!*) And it not only has this right, it has a duty to protect itself. (*Commotion among the Social Democrats.*) No army in the world can exist otherwise. (*Quite right! from the Right.*) The King's uniform must be respected under all circumstances. (*Lively agreement on the Right. Interjection by the Social Democrats. Long, widespread commotion.*) And gentlemen, I have no doubt that it was solely the consciousness of this duty to protect the army which caused the military authorities in Zabern to intervene, even if, as a consequence, because of the measures taken, legal restrictions were not observed. (*Hear! Hear! from the Social Democrats.*)

Verhandlungen des Reichstages (1913), vol. 291, p. 6155.

The case for a large battle fleet

In his 1897 memorandum for William II, Tirpitz made clear the anti-British thrust of his naval programme.

2. For Germany the most dangerous naval enemy at the present time is England. It is also the enemy against which we most urgently require a certain measure of force as a political power factor.
3. Commerce raiding and transatlantic war against England is so

hopeless, because of the shortage of bases on our side and the superfluity on England's side, that we must ignore this type of war against England in our plans for the constitution of our fleet.

4. Our fleet must be so constructed that it can unfold its greatest military potential between Heligoland and the Thames. . . .

6. The military situation against England demands battleships in as great a number as possible. . . .

Steinberg (**144**), p. 208.

document 25

The navy as focus for nationalism

The press bureau of the Imperial Navy Office funded a wide variety of propaganda; this article claimed to demonstrate the advantages for the working class in a strong battle fleet.

. . . the concept of the navy has indeed, as *Prince Bismarck* once said, been the hearth around which the German attempts at unity have clustered and warmed themselves. Thus it has already helped to fulfil a great national mission. It has also, however, been allotted the further task of overcoming the discord between the parties in the united German Empire, and directing the minds of the disputants towards a higher goal: the greatness and glory of the Fatherland. Today millions of our compatriots are spiritually alienated from the state and the prevailing economic order; the concept of the navy possesses the power – that we have nowadays perceived – to revive the national spirit of the classes and fill them once again with patriotic loyalty and love for Kaiser and Reich.

Nauticus, *Jahrbuch für Deutschlands Seeinteressen* (1900), p. 225.

document 26

Reservations about the navy

Bülow, as this letter to Tirpitz at the end of 1908 shows, was beginning to realise the damage the navy was doing Germany's position.

. . . Your Excellency . . . refrains from expressing an opinion as to whether, in view of the present great superiority, which you yourself have emphasised, of the British fleet over our own naval forces – a superiority, moreover, which the British people appear resolved to maintain at all costs for the foreseeable future – it would be at all possible for our battleships to take a decisive part in hostilities in the event of a war with Britain. If, however, the fear is justified that our fleet, in its present strength, would be *kept blockaded in our harbours* by the overwhelming British naval forces, we have to reckon with the probability of being forced permanently on the *defensive* in a naval war with Britain. Thus the question arises whether it is not advisable, instead of concentrating exclusively on increasing the number of battleships, to turn our attention to the improvement of our coastal fortifications and the enlargement of our stock of underwater mines and the creation of a strong submarine fleet. . . .

. . . I believe . . . that considerations of a political nature make it advisable to entertain the question whether a slowing down in the implementation of the current naval programme should not be seriously considered.

Alfred von Tirpitz, *Politische Dokumente*, vol. 1 (Stuttgart and Berlin, 1924), p. 101.

A 'place in the sun'

document 27

In a speech to the Reichstag in December 1897, Bülow justified the acquisition of Kiaochow as well as an incident in Haiti, and laid down the guidelines of Weltpolitik.

. . . The times when the German left the land to one of his neighbours, the sea to the other, and reserved heaven, where pure doctrine is enthroned, for himself (*Laughter – Bravo!*) – those times are past. We regard it as one of our foremost duties, specifically in East Asia, to further and cultivate our shipping, our trade and our industry.

. . . We must demand that the German missionary and the German trader, German goods, the German flag and German ships in China are just as much respected as those of other powers. (*Lively Bravos!*) Finally we are perfectly prepared to take account of the interests of other great powers, in the certain prospect that our own interests will meet with the same recognition they deserve. (*Bravo!*) In short: we don't want to put anyone in the shade, but we demand our place in the sun too. (*Bravo!*) In East Asia as in the West Indies we will endeavour to safeguard our rights and our interests, true to the traditions of German policy, without unnecessary severity, but also without weakness. (*Lively applause.*)

Fenske (**2**), pp. 132–3.

An advocate of both *Weltpolitik* and *Lebensraum*

General Bernhardi is better known for recommending a preventive war; but his popular book was also an attempt to reconcile the two main strands of German imperialism.

We are absolutely dependent on foreign countries for the import of raw materials, and to a considerable extent also for the sale of our own manufactures. We even obtain a part of our necessaries of life from abroad. Then, again, we have not the assured markets which England possesses in her colonies. Our own colonies are unable to take much of our products, and the great foreign economic spheres try to close their doors to outsiders, especially Germans. . . . The livelihood of our working classes directly depends on the maintenance and expansion of our export trade. It is a question of life and death for us to keep open our overseas commerce. We shall very soon see ourselves compelled to find for our growing population means of life other than industrial employment. It is out of the question that this latter can keep pace permanently with the increase of population. Agriculture will employ a small part of this increase, and home settlements may afford some relief. But no remunerative occupation will ever be found within the borders of the existing German Empire for the whole population, however favourable our international relations. We shall soon, therefore, be faced by the question, whether we wish to surrender the coming generations to foreign countries, as formerly in the hour of our decline, or whether we wish to take steps to find them a home in our own German colonies, and so retain them for the fatherland. There is no possible doubt how this question must be answered. If the unfortunate course of our history has hitherto prevented us from building a colonial Empire, it is our duty to make up for lost time, and at once to construct a fleet which, in defiance of all hostile Powers, may keep our sea communications open.

... In the future ... the importance of Germany will depend on two points: firstly, how many millions of men in the world speak German? secondly, how many of them are politically members of the German Empire?

F. von Bernhardi, *Germany and the Next War* (London, 1914 [1912]), pp. 82–3.

Germany as 'master of Europe' document 29

In 1911 the industrialist Hugo Stinnes claimed that informal, economic hegemony was more effective than a noisy and aggressive foreign policy.

He talked about how wrong it was to look upon externally visible attributes of power as decisive. He relied much more on *economic* power. 'And see what it means when I slowly but surely acquire the majority of shares in this or that company; when I little by little pick up more and more of Italy's coal supply; when I unobtrusively gain a foothold in Sweden and Spain for essential minerals; when I even establish myself in Normandy – give us another 3–4 years of peaceful development, and Germany will be the undisputed master of Europe. We have left the French behind us; they're a nation of small-time investors. And the British aren't hard-working enough and don't have the daring for new enterprises. Otherwise there is no one in Europe who could compete with us. So: 3 or 4 years of peace, and I personally will guarantee German hegemony in Europe on the quiet.'

Heinrich Class, *Wider den Strom: Vom Werden und Wachsen der nationalen Opposition im alten Reich* (Leipzig, 1932), p. 217.

'Encirclement' document 30

(a) *Count Schlieffen's influence did not end with his retirement. In a 1909 article, with which Moltke agreed wholeheartedly, and which the Emperor read out to his generals, Schlieffen conjured up a vision of a Germany ringed by enemies.*

In the centre stand Germany and Austria, unprotected, around them, behind wall and moat, the other powers. The military situation is analogous to the political one. Between the encircling and the encircled powers exist almost insuperable differences. . . .

We cannot say for certain whether this emotion and covetousness will transform itself into violent action. But strenuous efforts are nevertheless being made to bring all these powers together for a joint attack on the centre. At the given moment the gates will be opened, the drawbridges let down, and the million-strong armies will flood in over the Vosges, the Meuse, the Königsau, the Niemen, the Bug and even over the Isonzo and the Tirolese Alps, ravaging and destroying. The danger seems gigantic.

Alfred von Schlieffen, *Gesammelte Schriften*, vol. 1 (Berlin, 1913), pp. 20–1.

(**b**) *At the height of the July Crisis in 1914, William II made a marginal comment on a report which showed how strong the encirclement complex was, even if his historical analysis, blaming everything on Edward VII, was thoroughly inaccurate.*

. . . Frivolity and weakness are to plunge the world into the most frightful war, which eventually aims at the destruction of Germany. For I have no doubt left about it: England, Russia and France have *agreed* among themselves . . . to take the Austro-Serbian conflict for an *excuse* for waging a *war of extermination against* us. . . .

. . . That is the real naked situation . . . which, slowly and cleverly set going, certainly by Edward VII, has been carried on, and systematically built up by disowned conferences between England and Paris and St Petersburg; finally brought to a conclusion by George V and set to work. And thereby the stupidity and ineptitude of our ally is turned into a snare for us. So the famous 'encirclement' of Germany has finally become a complete fact, despite every effort of our politicians and diplomats to prevent it. The net has been suddenly thrown over our head, and England sneeringly reaps the most brilliant success of her persistently prosecuted purely *anti-German world-policy*, against which we have proved ourselves helpless, while she twists the noose of our political and economic destruction out of our fidelity to Austria, as we squirm *isolated* in the net. A great achievement, which arouses the admiration even of him who is to be destroyed as its result! Edward VII is stronger after his death than am I who am still alive!

Geiss (**3**), pp. 294–5.

document 31

Bethmann Hollweg's *Weltpolitik*

In a Memorandum of 1910, the Chancellor showed that colonial expansion and the fleet were still very much part of imperial policy.

The Imperial Chancellor wants a brief note, which shows that, since his taking up office, there has been no deviation from the lines which have obtained up to now and which were laid down by by his predecessors, especially in the sense of softness towards foreign powers... *England*: Continuation of previous policy. Understanding over a few African questions, readiness for further such understandings. Alteration of our Navy Law out of the question.

Zentrales Staatsarchiv (AA/4615), Potsdam.

document 32

The question of British neutrality

On 4 June 1914 the Bavarian representative in Berlin reported on a conversation with the Chancellor which revealed how clearly Bethmann Hollweg saw the constraints on foreign governments.

... he discussed ... the general political situation, and this time, in fact, which I want to emphasise particularly, in a thoroughly unoptimistic manner. Herr von Bethmann has not been able to alter the basic tendency of British and Russian policy towards us. ... So despite repeated attempts Herr von Bethmann has not succeeded in concluding a treaty of neutrality with Britain, and as for Russia, his handling of the appointment of General Liman in Turkey has shown as clearly as possible how few concessions Germany can count on in St Petersburg where it is a question of vital concerns of Russian policy. ...

As far as Britain is concerned, his remarks ran roughly as follows: British power has always, at all times, stood against the strongest power on the Continent. First against Spain, then against France, later against Russia, now against Germany. Britain does not want war. He – the Chancellor – knows for certain that the British government has repeatedly declared to Paris that it would be associated with no provocative policy and no aggressive war against Germany. But that would not prevent us, if it came to war, from finding Britain not on our side. Whether his predecessor had not missed coming to an understanding with England . . . he is willing to overlook. Britain had offered her services – that much was clear – but he still thinks that even then British friendship was only to be had at the price of Germany not building a strong navy. . . .

The danger hardly threatened from France. . . . they don't want war in France. Russia is more dangerous. There, Slav frenzy could turn heads so much that one day Russia might commit stupidities.

P. Dirr (ed.), *Bayerische Dokumente zum Kriegsausbruch* . . . , 2nd edit. (Munich, 1924), pp. 111–13.

document 33

Splitting the Entente or world war

(a) *The Diary of Bethmann Hollweg's secretary Kurt Riezler is a crucial guide to German strategy in July 1914.*

7.7.1914
The secret information which he [the Chancellor] imparts to me conveys a disturbing picture. He regards the Anglo-Russian negotiations over a naval convention . . . very seriously, last link in the chain. . . .

The Chancellor talks of difficult decisions. Murder of Francis Ferdinand. Official Serbia involved. Austria wants to bestir herself. Message of Francis Joseph to the Emperor enquiring about *casus foederis*. Our old dilemma in every Austrian move in the Balkans. If we encourage them, they will say we pushed them into it; if we try to dissuade them, then we're supposed to have left them in the lurch. Then they turn to the western powers whose arms are open, and we lose our last halfway reliable ally. This time it's worse than 1912; for this time Austria is on the defensive against the subversive activities of Serbia and Russia. A move against Serbia can lead to world war. The Chancellor expects a war, however it turns out, to lead to an overthrow of the whole existing order. . . . The future belongs to Russia, which grows and grows and weighs upon us like a heavier and heavier nightmare.
8.7.14
If war comes from the East, so that we would come to Austria-Hungary's aid rather than Austria-Hungary coming to ours, we have a chance of winning it. If war does not come, if the Tsar does

not want it or if an alarmed France advises peace, then we still have
the prospect of manoeuvring the Entente apart over this move.

(b) *A further entry shows the importance of letting the Russians mobilise first.*

23.7.14
The Chancellor believes that if there is war it will be unleashed by
Russian mobilisation. . . . In this case there will be little to negotiate
about because we shall have to wage war immediately in order to
have a chance of winning. Yet the entire nation will then sense the
danger and rise in arms. . . .

Erdmann (**1**), pp. 182–4, 190.

The confidence of the army

document 34

The diary of General Wenninger, Bavarian military attaché *in Berlin, gives
some idea of the mood of impatient anticipation in army circles at the prospect
of war.*

29.7.1914
The [Bavarian] envoy . . . was sitting at breakfast in his bedroom.
He said that the wisdom of diplomacy would succeed in preserving
peace. I openly confessed myself one of those who would regard it
as a piece of good fortune if the God of the Germans were to thwart
all the arts of diplomacy.
31.7.1914
I hurry to the [Prussian] war ministry [upon the decision to
proclaim the period preceding mobilisation]. Beaming faces
everywhere, – people shaking hands in the corridors; we congratu-
late one another, that we are over the ditch.
1.8.1914
Then I hurried to the war ministry. The impatience was at boiling
point. We are losing a mobilisation day, while to the right and left
of us they are obviously mobilising smoothly. . . .

Schulte (**190**), pp. 137, 140–1.

Hopes of reparations

The German government, like the Allies, intended making Germany's enemies pay for the War, as Treasury Secretary Helfferich explained to the Reichstag in March 1915.

. . . the federated governments have believed themselves able to refrain, for the moment, from introducing war taxes. They have believed they should not make the heavy burdens already imposed on the country by war even heavier with new taxes or tax increases, as long as there is no necessity for it in the drafting of the imperial budget. They have been strengthened in this belief by the fact that even the severest taxation measures would be able to cover only a small percentage of our massive war costs, that moreover the present war is being waged not only for the present, but also above all for our future, and that we hold fast to the hope of being able, at the conclusion of peace, to present the bill for this war which has been forced upon us to our enemies.

An das deutsche Volk: Die Reichstagsreden des Kanzlers und des Schatzsekretärs zum Weltkrieg (Berlin, 1915), p. 63.

The power of the OHL

Bethmann Hollweg's downfall in July 1917 was the ultimate example of military interference in politics, described by a general staff officer.

We noticed the severe internal struggle going on in the Field Marshal [Hindenburg]. However, there could be no doubt that General Ludendorff would prevail. The latter was kept informed by Colonel Bauer in Berlin of further developments there, developments which Bauer decisively influenced.

I was deeply annoyed by all this, even enraged; and my anger was directed especially at – the Emperor. I held him primarily responsible for the confusion in which we were now. . . . The Emperor was a disappointment to *everybody*. And that was how things were supposed to go on.

General Ludendorff played his final trump against the imperial Chancellor. He submitted a request to be relieved of his wartime post, and – Hindenburg joined him. Whether with a heavy or a light heart plays no role here. It worked. The Emperor received the news about it over the telephone from Kreuznach . . . , he summoned both generals in a towering rage, but then found himself obliged to give way to Bethmann Hollweg's representations after all, which ran as follows: 'I can't stay, if the generals go.'

Wilhelm Deist (ed.), *Militär und Innenpolitik im Weltkrieg 1914-1918*, vol. 2 (Düsseldorf, 1970), p. 792.

document 37
'Moderate' war aims

In addition to Bethmann Hollweg's September Programme, other government plans were drafted, such as the October 1914 memorandum by the Prussian Minister of the Interior.

We are fighting for our world political future. To ensure it we naturally need above all an extensive territorial and alliance coverage on the Continent against attacks on the motherland, a security which in practical worth approximates that which Britain possesses because of the sea. This security calls for a lasting weakening of France and strengthening of our western frontier. It calls for an end to the special status of Belgium which has been shown to be untenable. It forbids a too far-reaching Slavicisation or Polonisation of Austria-Hungary. It forbids the emergence of any new neighbour bent upon revenging itself on us, in which all our rivals would find an ally against us. Lastly it makes it appear desirable that Britain as well as Japan should remain under a continuous pressure, which can only be exerted by a Russia which is at our beck and call. For since Russia is a power political reality which cannot be rationalised away, and we feel no need to enrich ourselves at its expense, we must see to it that we are able to make it useful for our world political interests.

Reichstag, *Die Ursachen des deutschen Zusammenbruches im Jahre 1918*, vol. 12/1: *Die Annexionsfragen des Weltkrieges* (Berlin, 1929), p. 193.

document 38

Bethmann Hollweg's *Mitteleuropa*

The Chancellor and many others believed in a central European economic union dominated by Germany. Two extracts from Riezler's diary show the persistence of this thinking.

19.8.[1914]
In the evening long conversation about Poland and the possibility of a loose joining of other states to the Empire – central European system of differential tariffs. Greater Germany with Belgium Holland Poland as close, Austria as loose, protectorates.

11.3.17
. . . the policy of the I[mperial] C[hancellor], to lead the German Empire – which by the methods of the Prussian territorial state, alone in the middle of Europe, cannot become a world power, and probably is only tenable at all for a limited period – into an imperialism of European gestures, to organise the continent from the centre outwards (Austria Poland Belgium) around our secret leadership – has made progress for a while, even if slowly. . . .

Erdmann (**1**), pp. 198, 416.

document 39

Extreme war aims

In a letter to the historian Hans Delbrück in 1915, Ludendorff was already thinking in terms of permanent expansion and war.

We must be a strong central Europe. The more we work to enlist people the better, like Holland, Sweden, perhaps Roumania.

The greatest difficulty is Austria. You know my views on that country. A gentle but iron hand will be needed to raise the country up militarily, economically. . . . Any growth in Poland's strength weakens Austria and is therefore to be rejected, which brings me to my solution for the Polish and eastern question especially.

A partition and domination is necessary here too, so: Polish Kingdom without Suwalki an autonomous state; the other parts, and indeed as much as possible, for Prussia. Here we gain breeding grounds for men, which are necessary for further struggles in the East. The latter will come, inevitably.

In the West I am unconditionally in favour of the seizure of the coal basin of Briey and if at all possible the gaining of Belfort; France must be made to feel that it has been beaten. Belgium must be closely joined to us, without entering the imperial federation. . . . Annexation of Belgium leads us to Holland, and there I see a further need for incorporating Belgium. Together with Holland and its harbours [we have] the basis for a naval war with Britain.

Thus augmented in strength . . . we can see whether Britain or Russia will not seek association with us. If we succeed in winning over Japan as well, then we have the position we need. . . .

Zechlin (**230**), pp. 352–3.

document 40

Public morale and war-weariness

(a) *The Spartakus League was one of the few consistent anti-war voices. A pamphlet of 1916 highlighted the greatest problem for ordinary German citizens.*

What had to come, has happened: Starvation!

In Leipzig, in Berlin, in Charlottenburg, in Braunschweig, in Magdeburg, in Koblenz and Osnabrück, in many other places, there are riots of starving crowds in front of shops for foodstuffs. And in the face of the starving cries of the masses the government of the state of siege has only one answer: heightened state of siege, police sabres and military patrols.

Mr von Bethmann Hollweg accuses Britain of the crime of being guilty of starvation in Germany, and those who want to see the War through to the bitter end, and the government's pimps, prattle on in the same sense. Nevertheless, the German government must have known that this would happen: war against Russia, France and Britain was bound to lead to the blockading of Germany. The War, genocide, is the crime, the aim of starving us out only a consequence of this crime.

(b) *Richard Stumpf was an ordinary seaman, patriotic and conservative-minded. His diary testified to the serious discontent in the navy as early as the summer of 1917.*

If I were called upon to pass judgment on the current mood of the crews, it would, like a doctor's diagnosis, go something like this: High degree of excitement, brought on by complete lack of confidence in the officers; persistence of the fixed idea that the War is being waged and prolonged only in the interests of the officers; and violent outbreaks of anger due to the fact that the crews are starving and suffering, while the officers are living high and rolling in money.

So is it any wonder if the men are finally grasping the infallible means of mutiny to improve their miserable lot?

(c) *A letter of January 1918, from a soldier on the western front, speaks for itself.*

Peace is probably not going to come after all. None of us gives a damn whether we get Courland or not, if only there were peace. Anyway after peace is concluded there will come a time so hard, harder than the whole War. I was a great idealist when I marched off to war, but I am bitterly disappointed. Don't imagine that we're going to keep silent about what we have seen and experienced. Things ought to, and must, get better in Germany. The Prussian officer shouldn't be the only person in the state.

But that is all a long way off. First let's just have peace, then comes the great reckoning.

Herbert Michaelis and Ernst Schraepler (eds), *Ursachen und Folgen vom deutschen Zusammenbruch 1918 und 1945 . . .* , vol. 1 (Berlin, n.d. [1960]), pp. 185, 226 and 242.

document 41
'Revolution from above'

Admiral von Hintze, Foreign Secretary in 1918, recorded after the War how the OHL approved Germany's parliamentarisation on 29 September.

I described the position of our allies: Bulgaria defected; Austria-Hungary's defection imminent; Turkey only an extra burden, no help; state of our peace initiative with Holland. . . .

General Ludendorff explained the military situation: . . . the condition of the army required immediate ceasefire in order to avert a catastrophe. . . .

As a way out of this situation I expounded: Gathering together *all* the nation's forces for defence in the final struggle.

As means I mentioned: 1. Dictatorship; the dictatorship would be tied to the condition that military successes, if not victory, could be promised in the foreseeable future, otherwise it would be followed by revolution or chaos;

2. Revolution from above; the sudden swing from confidence in victory to defeat must deal a blow to the nation, the consequences of which Empire and dynasty would hardly survive. To anticipate the shock, unleash a people's war, which would send the last man to the front – let the broadest possible circles be given an interest in the outcome by drawing them into the government.

3. To procure the immediate ceasefire, which the OHL demanded: an invitation to conclude peace *via* the President of the United States, on the basis of his published proposals.

General Ludendorff rejected dictatorship: Victory would be impossible, the state of the army demanded rather immediate ceasefire.

The Field Marshal [Hindenburg] and General Ludendorff approved the revolution from above. . . .

Reichstag, *Ursachen des deutschen Zusammenbruches . . . 1918*, vol. 2; *. . . Die politischen und militärischen Verantwortlichkeiten . . .* (Berlin, 1927), pp. 400–1.

The army shifts the blame   **document 42**

When Ludendorff conceded defeat on 29 September, he made it clear to his subordinates that the army could accept no share of the responsibility for what had happened. Colonel von Thaer was present.

Frightful and horrible! It's true! Really! When we were assembled, Ludendorff walked into our midst, his face full of deepest grief, pale, but with head held high. The true picture of a handsome, Germanic hero! I couldn't help thinking of Siegfried, with the mortal wound in his back from Hagen's spear. . . .

It had been a terrible moment for the Field Marshal and him [Ludendorff], to have to report this [Germany's defeat] to H[is] M[ajesty] and the Chancellor. The latter, Count Hertling, had told HM in dignified fashion that as a result he must thereupon lay down his office. . . .

Excellency Ludendorff added: 'At the moment therefore we do not have a Chancellor. Who it will be, is still unclear. *But I have asked HM to bring those circles into the government now, whom we have primarily to thank that we have got to this stage.* So we are going to let these gentlemen move into the ministries. They are going to have to conclude the peace, that now *has* to be concluded. They are going to have to eat the soup they have cooked for us!'

Albrecht von Thaer, *Generalstabsdienst an der Front und in der O.H.L: Aus Briefen und Tagebuchaufzeichnungen 1915–1919* (Göttingen, 1958), pp. 234–5.

Chronology

1871	German Empire founded
1888–1918	William II Emperor
1890	Bismarck dismissed
	Lapse of anti-socialist legislation
	Pan-German League founded
1890–94	Caprivi Chancellor
1892–94	Caprivi trade treaties
1893	Farmers' League founded
1894–1900	Hohenlohe Chancellor
1897–1916	Tirpitz navy secretary
1897	Acquisition of Kiaochow
1898	First Navy Law
1900–09	Bülow Chancellor
1900	Second Navy Law
1902	Bülow Tariff Law
1904–07	Herero revolt in South-West Africa
1907	Bülow Bloc formed
1908	*Daily Telegraph* affair
	Expropriation Law against Poles
1909	'Blue-Black' Bloc formed
1909–17	Bethmann Hollweg Chancellor
1911	Alsace-Lorraine constitution
1912	SPD becomes largest party in Reichstag
1912–13	Balkan Wars
1913	Large increases in army
	Zabern incident
1914	First World War begins
1916–18	Hindenburg Chief of the General Staff
1917	United States declares war on Germany
	Russian Revolution
1918	Treaty of Brest-Litovsk (March)
	Army admits defeat (September)
	Naval mutinies begin (October)
	German republic proclaimed in Berlin (9 November)
	Armistice ends War (11 November)
1919	Treaty of Versailles

Glossary

ADV (Alldeutscher Verband)   Pan-German League 1891–1939 (informally launched 1890).

BdI (Bund der Industriellen)   Industrialists' League 1895–1919. Light manufacturers, against high tariffs.

BdL (Bund der Landwirte)   Farmers' League 1893–1920. Extreme agrarians (landowners and small farmers), for high tariffs.

CVDI (Centralverband deutscher Industriellen)   Central Association of German Industrialists 1876–1919. Heavy industrialists, for high tariffs.

DFP (Deutsche Freisinnige Partei)   German Free Thought Party 1884–93. Left-liberal; split into three factions 1893–1910; reunited as

FVP (Fortschrittliche Volkspartei)   Progressive People's Party 1910–18.

DKP (Deutschkonservative Partei)   German Conservative Party 1876–1918.

DLR (Deutscher Landwirtschaftsrat)   German Agricultural Council. Moderate agrarians.

DVP (Deutsche Vaterlandspartei)   German Fatherland Party 1917–18. Extreme annexationist. Leaders: A. von Tirpitz; Wolfgang Kapp.

Guelphs   Party for an independent Hanover 1869–1933.

HKT   German Eastern Marches Society 1894–1935. Extreme nationalist settlement pressure group. Known as *Hakatisten* after initials of founding leaders Hansemann, Kennemann and Tiedemann.

KRA (Kriegsrohstoffabteilung)   War Raw Materials Section.

Landtag   Parliament of a federated state, e.g. Prussia.

Lebensraum   Literally, 'living space'; used to describe expansionist aims in eastern Europe.

Mitteleuropa   Central Europe; idea of an economic union dominated by Germany.

National Liberal Party   1867–1918. Upper and middle class, more national than liberal by 1890.

OHL (Oberste Heeresleitung)   Supreme Army Command.

Reichspartei   Imperial Party 1867–1918; originally Free Conservative Party (after 1871 only in Prussia). Moderate conservatives, pro-government.

Sammlungspolitik Policy of rallying the public, usually upper and middle classes, against socialism.

SKL (Seekriegsleitung) Naval War Command.

SPD (Sozialdemokratische Partei Deutschlands) German Social Democratic Party, 1875 to present.

Staatsstreich Forceful government action involving rule by extra-constitutional means.

TDN (Towarzystwo Demokratyczno-Narodowe) National Democratic Society 1909–18. Polish nationalist party.

USPD (Unabhängige sozialdemokratische Partei Deutschlands) Independent German Social Democratic Party 1917–22. Anti-war faction of SPD.

Weltpolitik World policy.

Wilhelmine Term used to describe period 1890–1918, i.e. that of William II's rule.

Zentrum German Centre Party 1870–1933. For defence of Catholic interests; broadly conservative.

Reichstag Election Results, 1890–1918

Name of party	Number of seats obtained in:					
	1890	1893	1898	1903	1907	1912
German Conservatives	73	72	56	54	60	43
Free Conservatives	20	28	23	21	24	14
National Liberals	42	53	46	51	54	45
Centre	106	96	102	100	105	91
Left-Liberals	76	48	49	36	49	42
Social Democrats	35	44	56	81	43	110
Poles	16	19	14	16	20	18
Danes	1	1	1	1	1	1
Alsace-Lorrainers	10	8	10	9	7	9
Guelphs	11	7	9	6	1	5
Anti-Semites	5	16	13	11	16	3
Others	2	5	18	11	17	16
Total	397	397	397	397	397	397

Source: Huber (5), vol. 2, pp. 538–9.

Bibliography

PRIMARY SOURCES

1 Erdmann, K. D., (ed.), *Kurt Riezler: Tagebücher–Aufsätze– Dokumente*, Göttingen, 1972.

2 Fenske, Hans, (ed.), *Unter Wilhelm II. 1890–1918: Quellen zum politischen Denken der Deutschen im 19. und 20. Jahrhundert*, Darmstadt, 1982.

3 Geiss, Imanuel, (ed.), *July 1914: The Outbreak of the First World War: Selected Documents*, London, 1967.

4 Görlitz, Walter, (ed.), *The Kaiser and his Court: The Diaries, Notebooks and Letters of Admiral Georg Alexander von Müller, Chief of the Naval Cabinet 1914–1918*, London, 1961 [1959].

5 Huber, Ernst Rudolf, (ed.), *Dokumente zur deutschen Verfassungsgeschichte*, 3 vols, Stuttgart, 1961–66.

6 Ritter, Gerhard A. and Jürgen Kocka (eds), *Deutsche Sozialgeschichte: Dokumente und Skizzen*, vol. II: *1870–1914*. Munich, 1974.

7 Röhl, John C. G., (ed.), *From Bismarck to Hitler: The Problem of Continuity in German History*, London, 1970.

STUDIES OF THE KAISER

8 Cecil, Lamar, *William II: Prince and Emperor, 1859–1900*, Chapel Hill, N. C., and London, 1989.

9 Hull, Isabel V., *The Entourage of Kaiser Wilhelm II 1888–1918*, Cambridge, 1982.

10 Röhl, John C. G., *Kaiser, Hof und Staat: Wilhelm II und die deutsche Politik*, Munich, 1987.

11 Röhl, John C. G., 'The Emperor's New Clothes: A Character Sketch of Kaiser Wilhelm II', in (**12**).

12 Röhl, John C. G. and Nicolaus Sombart (eds), *Kaiser Wilhelm II: New Interpretations*, Cambridge, 1982.

GENERAL HISTORIES

13 Berghahn, Volker R., *Germany and the Approach of War in 1914*, London and Basingstoke, 1973.

14 Berghahn, Volker R., *Modern Germany: Society, Economy and Politics in the Twentieth Century*, Cambridge, 1982.

15 Blackbourn, David, *Populists and Patricians: Essays in Modᵉrn German History*, London, 1987.

16 Blackbourn, David and Geoff Eley, *The Peculiarities of German History: Bourgeois Society and Politics in Nineteenth-Century Germany*, Oxford and New York, 1984.

17 Blanning, T. C. W., 'The Death and Transfiguration of Prussia', *Historical Journal*, 29, 1986.

18 Böhme, Helmut, *Deutschlands Weg zur Grossmacht: Studien zum Verhältnis von Wirtschaft und Staat während der Reichsgründungszeit 1848–1881*, Cologne, 1966.

19 Carr, William, *A History of Germany 1815–1945*, 3rd edit., London, 1986.

20 Craig, Gordon A., *Germany 1866–1945*, Oxford, 1978.

21 Dukes, Jack R. and Joachim Remak, (eds), *Another Germany: A Reconsideration of the Imperial Era*, Boulder, Col., 1988.

22 Eley, Geoff, *From Unification to Nazism: Reinterpreting the German Past*, London, 1986.

23 Evans, Richard J., *Rethinking German History: Nineteenth Century Germany and the Origins of the Third Reich*, London, 1987.

24 Evans, Richard J., (ed.), *Society and Politics in Wilhelmine Germany*, London, 1978.

25 Fenske, Hans, *Deutsche Verfassungsgeschichte: Vom Norddeutschen Bund bis heute*, Berlin, 1981.

26 Fischer, Fritz, *From Kaiserreich to Third Reich: Elements of Continuity in German History 1871–1945*, London, 1986 [1979].

27 Frauendienst, Werner, Wolfgang J. Mommsen, Walther Hubatsch and Albert Schwarz, *Handbuch der deutschen Geschichte: Deutsche Geschichte der neuesten Zeit von Bismarcks Entlassung bis zur Gegenwart*, vol. IV, pt. 1: *Von 1890 bis 1933*, Frankfurt, 1973.

28 Hucko, Elmar M., *The Democratic Tradition: Four German Constitutions*, Leamington Spa, Hamburg and New York, 1987.

29 Kehr, Eckart, *Economic Interest, Militarism and Foreign Policy: Essays on German History*, ed. Gordon A. Craig, Berkeley, Los Angeles and London, 1977.

30 Kitchen, Martin, *The Political Economy of Germany 1815–1914*, London, 1978.

31 Koch, H. W., *A History of Prussia*, London and New York, 1978.

32 Koch, H. W., *A Constitutional History of Germany in the Nineteenth and Twentieth Centuries*, London, 1984.

33 Nipperdey, Thomas, 'Wehlers *Kaiserreich*: Eine kritische Auseinandersetzung', in *Gesellschaft, Kultur, Theorie: Gesammelte Aufsätze zur neuren Geschichte*, Göttingen, 1976.

34 Nipperdey, Thomas, *Nachdenken über die deutsche Geschichte*, Munich, 1986

35 Rosenberg, Arthur, *Imperial Germany: The Birth of the German Republic 1871–1918*, London, New York and Toronto, 1970 [1931].

36 Schöllgen, Gregor, 'Griff nach der Weltmacht? 25 Jahre Fischer-Kontroverse', *Historisches Jahrbuch*, 106, 1986.

37 Sheehan, James J., 'The Primacy of Domestic Politics: Eckart Kehr's Essays on Modern German History', *Central European History*, 1, 1968.

38 Stern, Fritz, *The Failure of Illiberalism: Essays on the Political Culture of Modern Germany*, London, 1972.

39 Wehler, Hans-Ulrich, *Krisenherde des Kaiserreichs 1871–1918*, Göttingen, 1970.

40 Wehler, Hans-Ulrich, *The German Empire 1871–1918*, Leamington Spa and Dover, N.H., 1985 [1973].

DOMESTIC POLITICS

41 Barkin, Kenneth D., *The Controversy over German Industrialization 1890–1902*, Chicago and London, 1970.

42 Blackbourn, David, *Class, Religion and Local Politics in Wilhelmine Germany: The Centre Party in Württemberg before 1914*, New Haven, Conn., 1980.

43 Cole, Terence F., 'The *Daily Telegraph* Affair and its Aftermath: The Kaiser, Bülow and the Reichstag 1908–1909', in (**12**).

44 Crothers, George Dunlap, *The German Elections of 1907*, New York, 1968 [1941].

45 Dorpalen, Andreas, *Heinrich von Treitschke*, New Haven, Conn., 1975.

46 Eley, Geoff, *Reshaping the German Right: Radical Nationalism and Political Change after Bismarck*, New Haven, Conn., and London, 1980.

47 Eley, Geoff, 'Some Thoughts on the Nationalist Pressure Groups in Imperial Germany', in (**102**).

48 Epstein, Klaus, *Matthias Erzberger and the Dilemma of German Democracy*, Princeton, N. J., 1959.

49 Eyck, Erich, *Das persönliche Regiment Wilhelms II: Politische Geschichte des deutschen Kaiserreichs von 1890 bis 1914*, Erlenbach-Zürich, 1948.

50 Fraley, J. David, 'Government by Procrastination: Chancellor Hohenlohe and Kaiser Wilhelm II 1894–1900', *Central European History*, 7, 1974.

51 Gall, Lothar, *Bismarck: The White Revolutionary*, 2 vols, London, 1986–87 [1980].

52 Gellately, Robert, *The Politics of Economic Despair: Shopkeepers and German Politics 1890–1914*, Beverly Hills, Ca., 1974.

53 Hunt, James C., 'Peasants, Grain Tariffs and Meat Quotas: Imperial German Protectionism Reexamined', *Central European History*, 7, 1974.

54 Hunt, James C., *The People's Party in Württemberg and Southern Germany 1890–1914: The Possibilities of Democratic Politics*, Stuttgart, 1975.

55 Jarausch, Konrad H., *The Enigmatic Chancellor: Bethmann Hollweg and the Hubris of Imperial Germany*, New Haven, Conn., and London, 1973.

56 Kaelble, Hartmut, *Industrielle Interessenpolitik in der Wilhelminischen Gesellschaft: Centralverband Deutscher Industriellen 1895–1914*, Berlin, 1967.

57 Lerman, Kathy, 'The Decisive Relationship: Kaiser Wilhelm II and Chancellor Bernhard von Bülow 1900–1909', in (**12**).

58 Levy, Richard, *The Downfall of the Anti-Semitic Political Parties in Imperial Germany*, New Haven, Conn., 1975.

59 Lidtke, V., *The Outlawed Party: Social Democracy in Germany 1878–1890*, Princeton, N.J., 1966.

60 Maehl, W. H., *August Bebel: Shadow Emperor of the German Workers*, Philadelphia, 1980.

61 Miller, Susanne and Heinrich Potthoff, *A History of German Social Democracy from 1848 to the Present*, Leamington Spa, 1986.

62 Nichols, J. Alden, *Germany after Bismarck: The Caprivi Era 1890–1894*, New York, 1968 [1958].

63 Peck, Abraham J., *Radicals and Reactionaries: The Crisis of Conservatism in Wilhelmine Germany*, Washington, 1978.

64 Puhle, Hans Jürgen, *Agrarische Interessenpolitik und preussischer Konservatismus im Wilhelminischen Reich: Ein Beitrag zur Analyse des Nationalismus in Deutschland am Beispiel des Bundes der Landwirte und der Deutschkonservativen Partei 1893–1914*, Hanover, 1966.

65 Pulzer, Peter, *The Rise of Political Anti-Semitism in Germany and Austria*, 2nd edit., London, 1988 [1964].

66 Retallack, James N., *Notables of the Right: The Conservative Party and Political Mobilization in Germany 1876–1918*, London, 1989.

67 Röhl, J. C. G., *Germany without Bismarck: The Crisis of Government in the Second Reich 1890–1900*, London, 1967.

68 Ross, Ronald J., *The Beleaguered Tower: The Dilemma of Political Catholicism in Wilhelmine Germany*, Notre Dame, Ind., 1976.

69 Schoenbaum, David, *Zabern 1913: Consensus Politics in Imperial Germany*, London, 1982.

70 Sheehan, James· L., 'Leadership in the German Reichstag 1871–1918', *American Historical Review*, 74, 1968.

71 Sheehan, James L., *German Liberalism in the Nineteenth Century*, London, 1982 [1978].

72 Smith, Woodruff D. and Sharon A. Turner, 'Legislative Behaviour in the German Reichstag 1898–1906', *Central European History*, 14, 1981.

73 Stegmann, Dirk, *Die Erben Bismarcks: Parteien und Verbände in der Spätphase des Wilhelminischen Deutschland: Sammlungspolitik 1897–1918*, Berlin, 1970.

74 Struve, Walter, *Elites against Democracy: Leadership Ideals in Bourgeois Political Thought in Germany 1890–1933*, Princeton, N.J., 1973.

75 Suval, Stanley, *Electoral Politics in Wilhelmine Germany*, Chapel Hill, N.C., 1985.

76 Tirrell, Sarah R., *German Agrarian Politics after Bismarck's Fall: The Formation of the Farmers' League*, New York, 1951.

77 Weitowitz, R., *Deutsche Politik und Handelspolitik unter Reichskanzler Leo von Caprivi 1890–1894*, Düsseldorf, 1974.

78 White, Daniel, *The Splintered Party: National Liberalism in Hessen and the Reich 1867–1918*, Cambridge, Mass., 1976.

79 Williamson, D. G., *Bismarck and Germany 1862–1890*, London and New York, 1986.

80 Williamson, John G., *Karl Helfferich 1872–1924: Economist, Financier, Politician*, Princeton, N.J., 1971.

81 Witt, Peter-Christian, *Die Finanzpolitik des Deutschen Reiches von 1903 bis 1913: Eine Studie zur Innenpolitik des Wilhelminischen Deutschland*, Lübeck and Hamburg, 1970.

ECONOMIC AND SOCIAL HISTORY

82 Bade, Klaus J., (ed.), *Populism, Labour and Immigration in 19th and 20th Century Germany*, Leamington Spa, 1986.

83 Barkin, Kenneth D., 'Conflict and Concord in Wilhelmian Social Thought', *Central European History*, 5, 1972.

84 Blanke, Richard, *Prussian Poland in the German Empire (1871–1900)*, Boulder, Co., 1981.

85 Born, Karl Erich, *Staat und Sozialpolitik seit Bismarcks Sturz: Ein Beitrag zur Geschichte der innenpolitischen Entwicklung des Deutschen Reiches 1890–1914*, Wiesbaden, 1957.

86 Born, Karl Erich, *Wirtschafts- und Sozialgeschichte des Deutschen Kaiserreichs 1867/71–1914*, Stuttgart, 1985.

87 Chickering, Roger, *We Men Who Feel Most German: A Cultural Study of the Pan-German League 1886–1914*, Boston, London and Sydney, 1984.

88 Crew, David F., *Town in the Ruhr: A Social History of Bochum 1860–1914*, New York, 1979.

89 Evans, Richard J., *The Feminist Movement in Germany 1894–1933*, London and Beverly Hills, 1976.

90 Evans, Richard J., (ed.), *The German Working Class 1888–1933: The Politics of Everyday Life*, London, 1982.

91 Evans, Richard J., *Death in Hamburg: Society and Politics in the Cholera Years 1830–1910*, Oxford, 1987.

92 Evans, Richard J. and W. R. Lee (eds), *The German Peasantry: Conflict and Community from the Eighteenth to the Twentieth Centuries*, London, 1986.

93 Field, Geoffrey, *Evangelist of Race: The Germanic Vision of Houston Stewart Chamberlain*, New York, 1981.

94 Gasman, Daniel, *The Scientific Origins of National Socialism: Social Darwinism in Ernst Haeckel and the German Monist League*, New York and London, 1971.

95 Hagen, William, *Germans, Poles and Jews: The Nationality Conflict in the Prussian East 1772–1914*, Chicago, 1980.

96 Hauser, Oswald, 'Obrigkeitsstaat und demokratisches Prinzip im Nationalitätenkampf: Preussen im Nordschleswig', *Historische Zeitschrift*, 192, 1969.

97 Henderson, W. O., *The Industrial Revolution on the Continent: Germany France, Russia 1800–1914*, 2nd edit., London, 1967 [1961].

98 Henderson, W. O., *The Rise of German Industrial Power 1834–1914*, London, 1975.

99 Hickey, S. H. F., *Workers in Imperial Germany: The Miners of the Ruhr*, London, 1985.

100 Jarausch, Konrad H., *Students, Society and Politics in Imperial Germany: The Rise of Academic Illiberalism*, Princeton, N.J., 1982.

101 Kelly, Alfred, *The Descent of Darwin: The Popularization of Darwinism in Germany 1860–1914*, Chapel Hill, N.C., 1981.

102 Kennedy, Paul and Anthony Nicholls (eds), *Nationalist and Racialist Movements in Britain and Germany before 1914*, London, 1981.

103 Klessmann, Christoph, *Polnische Bergarbeiter im Ruhrgebiet 1870–1945: Soziale Integration und nationale Subkultur einer Minderheit in der deutschen Industriegesellschaft*, Göttingen, 1978.

104 Kulczycki, J., *School Strikes in Prussian Poland*, Boulder, Col., 1981.

105 Lebovics, Herman, *Social Conservatism and the Middle Classes in Germany 1914–1933*, Princeton, N. J., 1969.

106 Lidtke, Vernon L., *The Alternative Culture: Socialist Labor in Imperial Germany*, New York and Oxford, 1985.

107 Maschke, Eric, 'An Outline of the History of German Cartels from 1875 to 1914', in F. Crouzet, W. H. Chaloner and W. M. Stern (eds), *Essays in European Economic History 1789–1914*, New York, 1969.

108 Milward, Alan S. and S. B. Saul, *The Development of the Economies of Continental Europe 1850–1914*, London, 1977.

109 Moeller, Robert G., (ed.), *Peasants and Lords in Modern Germany: Recent Studies in Agricultural History*, Boston, Mass., London and Sydney, 1986.

110 Mommsen, Wolfgang J. and H.-G. Husung (eds), *The Development of Trade Unionism in Great Britain and Germany 1880–1914*, London, 1985.

111 Moses, John A., *German Trade Unionism from Bismarck to Hitler*, 2 vols, London, 1981.

112 Mosse, George L., *The Crisis of German Ideology: Intellectual Origins of the Third Reich*, New York, 1964.

113 Mosse, Werner E., *Jews in the German Economy: The German-Jewish Economic Elite 1820–1935*, Oxford, 1987.

114 Mosse, Werner E., *The German-Jewish Economic Elite 1820–1935: A Socio-Cultural Profile*, Oxford, 1989.

115 Neuburger, Hugh M., *German Banks and German Economic Growth 1871–1914*, London, 1975.

116 Perkins, J. A., 'The Agricultural Revolution in Germany 1850–1914', *Journal of European Economic History*, 10, 1981.

117 Ringer, Fritz K., *The Decline of the German Mandarins: The German Academic Community 1890–1933*, Cambridge, Mass., 1969.

118 Ritter, Gerhard A., *Social Welfare in Germany and Britain: Origins and Development*, Leamington Spa, 1986.

119 Röhl, John C. G., 'Higher Civil Servants in Germany 1890–1900', in James J. Sheehan (ed.), *Imperial Germany*, New York and London, 1976.

120 Sagarra, Eda, *An Introduction to Nineteenth Century Germany*, London, 1980.

121 Silverman, Dan P., *Reluctant Union: Alsace-Lorraine and Imperial Germany 1871–1918*, University Park, Pa., and London, 1972.

122 Spree, Reinhard, *Health and Social Class in Imperial Germany*, Leamington Spa, 1987.

123 Stern, Fritz, *The Politics of Cultural Despair: A Study in the Rise of the Germanic Ideology*, Berkeley, Ca., Los Angeles and London, 1974 [1961].

124 Tims, Richard Wonser, *Germanizing Prussian Poland: The H-K-T Society and the Struggle for the Eastern Marches in the German Empire 1894–1919*, New York, 1966 [1941].

125 Volkov, Shulamit, *Rise of Popular Antimodernization in Germany: The Urban Master Artisan 1873–1896*, Princeton, N.J., 1978.

126 Webb, Steven B., 'Agricultural Protection in Wilhelminian Germany: Forging an Empire with Pork and Rye', *Journal of Economic History*, 62, 1982.

127 Wertheimer, Jack, *Unwelcome Strangers: East European Jews in Imperial Germany*, New York and Oxford, 1987.

128 Winzen, Peter, 'Treitschke's Influence on the Rise of Imperialist and Anti-British Nationalism in Germany', in (**102**).

129 Woycke, James, *Birth Control in Germany 1871–1933*, London, 1988.

130 Zechlin, Egmont, *Die deutsche Politik und die Juden im Ersten Weltkrieg*, Göttingen, 1969.

MILITARY AND NAVAL HISTORY

131 Berghahn, Volker R., *Der Tirpitz-Plan: Genesis und Verfall einer innenpolitischen Krisenstrategie*, Düsseldorf, 1971.

132 Craig, Gordon A., *The Politics of the Prussian Army 1640–1945*, London, Oxford and New York, 1964 [1955].

133 Epkenhans, Michael, 'Grossindustrie und Schlachtflottenbau 1897–1914', *Militärgeschichtliche Mitteilungen*, 1/1988.

134 Granier, Gerhard, 'Deutsche Rüstungspolitik vor dem Ersten Weltkrieg: General Franz Wandels Tagebuchaufzeichnungen aus dem preussischen Kriegsministerium', *Militärgeschichtliche Mitteilungen*, 2/1985.

135 Herwig, Holger H., *The German Naval Officer Corps 1890–1981*, Oxford, 1973.

136 Herwig, Holger H., *'Luxury' Fleet: The Imperial German Navy 1888–1918*, London, 1980.

137 Kennedy, Paul M., 'Tirpitz, England and the Second Navy Law of 1900: A Strategical Critique', *Militärgeschichtliche Mitteilungen*, 2/1970.

138 Kitchen, Martin, *The German Officer Corps 1890–1914*, Oxford, 1968.

139 Lambi, Ivo Nikolai, *The Navy and German Power Politics 1862–1914*, Boston, London and Sydney, 1984.

140 Owen, Richard, 'Military-Industrial Relations: Krupp and the Imperial Navy Office', in (**24**).

141 Ritter, Gerhard, *The Schlieffen Plan*, London, 1958 [1956].

142 Ritter, Gerhard, *The Sword and the Sceptre: The Problem of Militarism in Germany*, 4 vols, London, 1972–3 [1954–68].

143 Schulte, Bernd F., *Europäische Krise und Erster Weltkrieg: Beiträge zur Militärpolitik des Kaiserreichs 1871–1914*, Frankfurt, 1983.

144 Steinberg, Jonathan, *Yesterday's Deterrent: Tirpitz and the Birth of the German Battle Fleet*, London, 1965.

145 Steinberg, Jonathan, 'The Tirpitz Plan', *Historical Journal, 16*, 1973.

146 Stone, Norman, 'Moltke-Conrad: Relations between the Austro-Hungarian and German General Staffs 1909–1914', *Historical Journal*, 9, 1966.

147 Weir, Gary E., 'Tirpitz, Technology and Building U-Boats 1897–1916', *International History Review*, 6, 1984.

FOREIGN AND COLONIAL POLICY

148 Bley, Helmut, *Southwest Africa under German Rule 1894–1914*, London, 1971 [1968].

149 Bridgman, Jon M., *The Revolt of the Hereros*, Berkeley, Ca., London, 1982.

150 Chickering, Roger, *Imperial Germany and a World without War: The Peace Movement and Germany Society 1892–1914*, Princeton, N.J., 1975.

151 Eley, Geoff, 'Defining Social Imperialism: Use and Abuse of an Idea', *Social History*, 1, 1976.

152 Fischer, Fritz, *World Power or Decline: The Controversy over 'Germany's Aims in the First World War'*, London, 1975 [1965].

153 Fischer, Fritz, *War of Illusions: German Policies from 1911 to 1914*, London, 1975 [1969].

154 Flannigan, M. L., 'German Economic Controls in Bulgaria: 1894–1914', *American Slavonic and East European Review*, 20, 1961.

155 Fletcher, Roger, *Revisionism and Empire: Socialist Imperialism in Germany 1897–1914*, London, 1984.

156 Geyer, Dietrich, *Russian Imperialism: The Interaction of Domestic and Foreign Policy 1860–1914*, Leamington Spa, 1987 [1977].

157 Hillgruber, Andreas, *Germany and the Two World Wars*, Cambridge, Mass. and London, 1981 [1967].

158 Iliffe, John, *Tanganyika under German Rule 1905–12*, Cambridge, 1969.

159 Jarausch, Konrad H., 'From Second Reich to Third Reich: The Problem of Continuity in German Foreign Policy', *Central European History*, 12, 1979.

160 Kennedy, Paul, *The Rise of the Anglo-German Antagonism 1860–1914*, London, 1980.

161 Langhorne, Richard, 'The Naval Question in Anglo-German Relations 1912–1914', *Historical Journal*, 14, 1971.

162 Lee, Marshall and Wolfgang Michalka, *German Foreign Policy 1917–1933: Continuity or Break?*, Leamington Spa, 1987.

163 Lorscheider, Horst M., 'The Commercial Treaty between Germany and Serbia of 1904', *Central European History*, 9, 1976.

164 Mommsen, Wolfgang J., 'Domestic Factors in German Foreign Policy before 1914', *Central European History*, 6, 1973.

165 Mommsen, Wolfgang J., *Max Weber and German Politics 1890–1920*, Chicago and London, 1984 [1959].

166 Moses, John A. and Paul M. Kennedy (eds), *Germany in the Pacific and Far East 1870–1914*, St Lucia, Queensland, 1977.

167 Pierard, Richard V., 'The German Colonial Society', in Arthur J. Knoll and Lewis H. Gann (eds), *Germans in the Tropics: Essays in German Colonial History*, New York, Westport, Conn., and London, 1987.

168 Rich, Norman, *Friedrich von Holstein: Politics and Diplomacy in the Era of Bismarck and Wilhelm II*, 2 vols, Cambridge, 1965.

169 Röhl, John C. G., 'An der Schwelle zum Weltkrieg: Eine Dokumentation über den "Kriegsrat" vom 8. Dezember 1912', *Militärgeschichtliche Mitteilungen*, 1/1977.

170 Schulte, Bernd F., 'Zu der Krisenkonferenz vom 8. Dezember 1912 in Berlin', *Historisches Jahrbuch*, 102, 1982.

171 Smith, Woodruff D., *The German Colonial Empire*, Chapel Hill, N.C., 1978.

172 Smith, Woodruff D., 'Friedrich Ratzel and the Origins of *Lebensraum*', *German Studies Review*, 3, 1980.

173 Smith, Woodruff D., *The Ideological Origins of Nazi Imperialism*, New York and Oxford, 1986.

174 Steinberg, Jonathan, 'Diplomatie als Wille und Vorstellung: Die Berliner Mission Lord Haldanes im Februar 1912', in H. Schottelius and W. Deist (eds), *Marine und Marinepolitik 1871– 1914*, Düsseldorf, 1972.

175 Steiner, Zara S., *Britain and the Origins of the First World War*, London and Basingstoke, 1977.

176 Stürmer, Michael, 'The German Dilemma: A Nation State against History and Geography', in Gregor Schöllgen (ed.), *Escape into War? The Foreign Policy of Imperial Germany*, Oxford, New York and Munich, 1990.

177 Wernecke, Klaus, *Der Wille zur Weltgeltung: Aussenpolitik und Öffentlichkeit am Vorabend des Ersten Weltkrieges*, Düsseldorf, 1970.

178 Winzen, Peter, 'Prince Bülow's *Weltmachtpolitik*', *Australian Journal of Politics and History*, 22, 1976.

179 Winzen, Peter, *Bülows Weltmachtkonzept: Untersuchungen zur Frühphase seiner Aussenpolitik 1897–1901*, Boppard am Rhein, 1977.

THE JULY CRISIS OF 1914

180 Bosworth, Richard, *Italy and the Approach of the First World War*, London, 1983.

181 Erdmann, K. D., 'War Guilt 1914 Reconsidered: A Balance of New Research', in (**187**).

182 Fischer, Fritz, 'World Policy, World Power and German War Aims', in (**187**).

183 Jarausch, Konrad H., 'The Illusion of Limited War: Chancellor Bethmann Hollweg's Calculated Risk, July 1914', *Central European History*, 2, 1969.

184 Joll, James, *The Origins of the First World War*, London and New York, 1984.

185 Kaiser, David E., 'Germany and the Origins of the First World War', *Journal of Modern History*, 55, 1983.

186 Keiger, John, *France and the Origins of the First World War*, London and Basingstoke, 1983.

187 Koch, H. W., (ed.), *The Origins of the First World War: Great Power Rivalry and German War Aims*, 2nd edit., London, 1984.

188 Lieven, D. C. B., *Russia and the Origins of the First World War*, Basingstoke and London, 1983.

189 Pogge von Strandmann, Hartmut, 'Germany and the Coming of War', in R. J. W. Evans and Hartmut Pogge von Strandmann (eds), *The Coming of the First World War*, Oxford, 1988.

190 Schulte, Bernd F., 'Neue Dokumente zu Kriegsausbruch und Kriegsverlauf 1914', *Militärgeschichtliche Mitteilungen*, 1/1979.

191 Zechlin, Egmont, 'Cabinet versus Economic Warfare in Germany: Policy and Strategy during the Early Months of the First World War', in (**187**).

THE FIRST WORLD WAR

192 Bucholz, Arden, *Hans Delbrück and the German Military Establishment: War Images in Conflict*, Iowa City, 1985.

193 Burchardt, Lothar, 'The Impact of the War Economy on the Civilian Population of Germany during the First and Second World Wars', in Wilhelm Deist (ed.), *The German Military in the Age of Total War*, Leamington Spa, 1985.

194 Conze, Werner E., *Polnische Nation und deutsche Politik im Ersten Weltkrieg*, Cologne, Graz, 1958.

195 Deist, Wilhelm, 'Die Politik der Seekriegsleitung und die Rebellion der Flotte Ende Oktober 1918', *Vierteljahrshefte für Zeitgeschichte*, 14, 1966.

196 Edwards, Marvin L., *Stresemann and the Greater Germany 1914–1918*, New York, 1963.

197 Farrar, L. L., *The Short War Illusion: German Policy, Strategy and Domestic Affairs August–December 1914*, Santa Barbara, Ca., and Oxford, 1973.

198 Farrar, L. L., *Divide and Conquer: German Efforts to Conclude a Separate Peace 1914–1918*, Boulder, Col., 1978.

199 Feldman, Gerald D., *Army, Industry and Labour 1914–1918*, Princeton, N. J., 1966.

200 Feldman, Gerald D., *Iron and Steel in the German Inflation 1916–1923*, Princeton, N. J., 1977.

201 Fischer, Fritz, *Germany's Aims in the First World War*, New York, 1967 [1961].

202 Gatzke, Hans W., *Germany's Drive to the West: A Study of Western War Aims during the First World War*, Baltimore, 1950.

203 Hill, Leonidas E., 'Signal zur Konterrevolution? Der Plan zum Vorstoss der deutschen Hochseeflotte am 30. Oktober 1918', *Vierteljahrshefte für Zeitgeschichte*, 36, 1988.

204 Horn, Daniel, *Mutiny on the High Seas: The Imperial German Naval Mutinies of World War One*, London, 1973 [1969].

205 Janssen, Karl Heinz, 'Der Wechsel in der Obersten Heeresleistung 1916', *Vierteljahrshefte für Zeitgeschichte*, 7, 1959.

206 Janssen, Karl Heinz, *Macht und Verblendung: Kriegszielpolitik der deutschen Bundesstaaten*, Göttingen, 1963.

207 Janssen, Karl Heinz, *Der Kanzler und der General: Die Führungskrise um Bethmann Hollweg und Falkenhayn 1914–1916*, Göttingen, 1967.

208 Kitchen, Martin, 'Militarism and the Development of Fascist Ideology: The Political Ideas of Colonel Max Bauer 1916–1918', *Central European History*, 7, 1975.

209 Kitchen, Martin, *The Silent Dictatorship: The Politics of the German High Command under Hindenburg and Ludendorff 1916–1918*, London, 1976.

210 Kocka, Jürgen, *Facing Total War: German Society 1914–1918*, Leamington Spa and Cambridge, Mass., 1984.

211 Kolb, Eberhard, (ed.), *Vom Kaiserreich zur Weimarer Republik*, Cologne, 1972.

212 Kolb, Eberhard, *The Weimar Republic*, London, 1988 [1984].

213 Lyth, Peter J., *Inflation and the Merchant Economy: The Hamburg Mittelstand 1914–1924*, Oxford, New York and Munich, 1990.

214 Matthias, Erich and Rudolf Morsey, 'Die Bildung der Regierung des Prinzen Max von Baden', in (**211**).

215 Meyer, Henry Cord, *Mitteleuropa in German Thought and Action 1815–1945*, The Hague, 1955.

216 Miller, Susanne, *Burgfrieden und Klassenkampf: Die deutsche Sozialdemokratie im Ersten Weltkrieg*, Düsseldorf, 1974.

217 Moeller, Robert E., 'Dimensions of Social Conflict in the Great War: The View from the German Countryside', *Central European History*, 14, 1981.

218 Mommsen, Wolfgang J., 'Die Regierung Bethmann Hollweg und die öffentliche Meinung 1914–1917', *Vierteljahrshefte für Zeitgeschichte*, 17, 1969.

219 Morgan, David W., *The Socialist Left and the German Revolution: A History of the German Independent Socialist Party 1917–1922*, Ithaca and New York, 1975.

220 Patemann, R., *Der Kampf um die preussische Wahlrechtsreform im Ersten Weltkrieg*, Düsseldorf, 1964.

221 Ryder, A. J., *The German Revolution of 1918: A Study of German Socialism in War and Revolt*, Cambridge, 1967.

222 Sauer, W., 'Das Scheitern der parlamentarischen Monarchie', in (**211**).

223 Schwabe, Klaus, 'Zur politischen Haltung der deutschen Professoren im Ersten Weltkrieg', *Historische Zeitschrift*, 193, 1961.

224 Stone, Norman, *The Eastern Front 1914–1917*, London, 1975.

225 Thompson, Wayne C., 'The September Program: Reflections on the Evidence', *Central European History*, 11, 1978.

226 Trotnow, Helmut, *Karl Liebknecht (1871–1919): A Political Biography*, New York, 1984 [1980].

227 Trumpener, Ulrich, *Germany and the Ottoman Empire 1914–1918*, Princeton, N. J., 1968.

228 Vincent, C. Paul, *The Politics of Hunger: The Allied Blockade of Germany 1915–1919*, Athens, Ohio and London, 1985.

229 Wheeler-Bennett, John W., *The Forgotten Peace: Brest-Litovsk March 1918*, New York, 1939.

230 Zechlin, Egmont, 'Ludendorff im Jahre 1915: Unveröffentlichte Briefe', in *Krieg und Kriegsrisiko: Zur deutschen Politik im Ersten Weltkrieg, Aufsätze*, Düsseldorf, 1979.

LATE ENTRIES

Lehman, Katharine Anne, *The Chancellor as Courtier: Bernhard von Bülow and the Governance of Germany 1900–1909*, Cambridge, 1990.

Mommsen, Wolfgang J., 'Kaiser Wilhelm II and German Politics', *Journal of Modern History*, 25, 1990.

Index